A WOMAN'S GUIDE TO

praying the scriptures

A BIBLE STUDY

PRAYERS FOR EVERY DAY
AND EVERY NEED

STORMIE OMARTIAN

HarperChristian Resources

A Woman's Guide to Praying the Scriptures

Published by HarperChristian Resources, 3950 Sparks Drive SE, Suite 101, Grand Rapids, MI 49546, USA.
HarperChristian Resources is a registered trademark of HarperCollins Christian Publishing, Inc.

Requests for information should be addressed to customercare@harpercollins.com.

ISBN 978-0-310-18016-6 (softcover)
ISBN 978-0-310-18017-3 (ebook)

[Content in this book has been adapted from *Praying God's Will for Your Life, Seven Prayers That Will Change Your Life Forever,* and *Lord, I Want to Be Whole.*]

This content is for inspirational and informational purposes only and is not a substitute for professional medical, psychological, or counseling advice; if you or someone you know is in crisis, please seek immediate help from a qualified healthcare professional.

HarperCollins Publishers, Macken House, 39/40 Mayor Street Upper, Dublin 1, D01 C9W8, Ireland (https://www.harpercollins.com).

Library of Congress Control Number: 2026936632

First Printing May 2026 / Printed in the United States
26 27 28 29 30 LBC 5 4 3 2 1

Contents

What You Need to Know Before You Start

Have you ever prayed for something and given up when God didn't answer quickly? Do you ever wonder if you are praying in a way that God will hear and answer? Are you comfortable persisting in prayer even when you see no evidence of an answer on the horizon? I've written this Bible study with these issues in mind.

Prayer has always been challenging, and the case could be made that we've got new obstacles to overcome. Our culture moves faster than ever before. We've grown accustomed to instant messaging, on-demand entertainment, fast food, and overnight shipping. We ask for things and receive them quickly. In the rare instances we must wait, we wonder if something has gone wrong. Without realizing it, it's possible to take these expectations to our prayer lives and then be sorely disappointed when God doesn't answer as quickly as we want Him to.

The truth is, God does hear and answer prayer. Keep in mind, God doesn't always answer on our timeline, and He sometimes answers in ways we wouldn't expect, but through the practice of prayer we deepen our relationship with Him and come to know Him in ways that can only happen by praying.

One of the most important things you can do to improve your prayer life is to learn to pray the Scriptures. Why? Because when you pray the Scriptures, you can be 100 percent confident that you are praying God's will over your life. Time and again you will be confronted with challenges, and sometimes it's difficult to know how to move forward. But if you know God's promises to you and understand what His Word says, you'll always know how to pray effectively. Will you get your prayers answered as quickly as you'd like? I can't promise you that. But based on the authority of God's Word I can tell you that praying God's Word is the best way forward. Isaiah 55:11 says,

> "So shall My word be that goes forth from My mouth;
> It shall not return to Me void,
> But it shall accomplish what I please,
> And it shall prosper in the thing for which I sent it."

This study is designed to guide you to the Scriptures and find out what God's Word says about specific situations. It is not to assume you will experience all of these situations, but if you do, you will know how to include Scripture in your prayers. As you study what the Bible says, you'll be prompted to use God's Word in your personal prayer time. My prayer for you is that this will become a lifelong practice. Remember, prayer and God's Word go hand in hand. Jesus said, "If you abide in Me, and My words abide in you, you will ask what you desire, and it shall be done for you" (John 15:7). What a wonderful promise from God!

May God bless you richly as you study His Word and seek Him in prayer. As a believer, there is no greater privilege.

With love for your journey,
Stormie Omartian
2026

A PRAYER TO
Know God's Will for Your Life

Do you ever wonder about God's will for your life? All of us want to make our days count and to avoid pitfalls that lead us in the wrong direction. In the days after I became a Christian I continually prayed, *God, tell me what to do. Show me what steps to take. Guide me where I need to go.* And God answered those prayers. He spoke to my heart, saying, *Just be in My presence. I'll make things happen the way they are supposed to.* In the following months and years, I learned that life could be much simpler than I ever dreamed.

It didn't matter what my situation was at the moment; all I had to do was take the next step the Lord was showing me. That was decades ago, and now I know that the will of God is not some mysterious thing that only a few select people can understand. It's there for each one of us, but we have to take the necessary steps to find it. The steps are simple, but often for that very reason we don't bother to take them. Yet we have to take them because we can never be happy until we understand God's will for our lives and are living in it. If you'll diligently seek God's will for your life, He will be faithful to show you.

Key Scripture

"I will instruct you and teach you in the way you should go . . ." (Psalm 32:8).

Prepare to Pray

If you want to know God's will for your life, it's important to be aware that God's will is most often found by reading the Bible. The Bible declares clearly that God has a definite will for each of our lives. Psalm 37:23 says, "The steps of a good man are ordered by the LORD." And in Psalm 32:8, God promises, "I will instruct you and teach you in the way you should go."

He speaks to us through His Word in the Scriptures. Second, God's will is continuous. From the time we are infants until the day we die, God has a will for us—as children, young people, adults, and senior citizens. Isaiah 58:11 says:

> "The LORD will guide you continually,
> And satisfy your soul in drought,
> And strengthen your bones;
> You shall be like a watered garden,
> And like a spring of water, whose waters do not fail."

God's will is specific. The prophet Isaiah heard the Lord promising His children, "Your ears shall hear a word behind you, saying, 'This is the way, walk in it,' whenever you turn to the right hand or whenever you turn to the left" (Isaiah 30:21).

And finally, God's will is profitable. The Lord told Joshua, who was to lead the Israelites into the promised land:

> "This Book of the Law shall not depart from your mouth, but you shall meditate in it day and night, that you may observe to do according to all that is written in it. *For then* you will make your way prosperous, and then you will have good success." (Joshua 1:8, emphasis added)

Study the Scriptures

- Make a list of the areas in your life that you're seeking God's guidance.

- Glance back at Isaiah 58:11. Practically speaking, what would it look like for God to "guide you continually" in these areas?

- The prophet Isaiah describes the person who is guided by the Lord as being like a "watered garden." What do you think Isaiah meant by this?

- Psalm 32:8 says, "I will instruct you and teach you in the way you should go." One of the primary ways God reveals His will is through His Word. Describe your Bible reading practices. Are there areas where you could improve? If so, what steps can you take to do so?

- Look up Joshua 1:8 in your Bible. The author describes talking about the Word, meditating on the Word, and obeying the Word. What is the outcome for someone who habitually does these things?

- Look up the following passages and consider how they relate to knowing God's will. How can you apply these truths to your own life?

Psalm 40:8	
Matthew 6:10	
Matthew 26:39	
Romans 12:2	
1 Thessalonians 4:3	

Respond to God's Word

Ultimately God's will for you is to make you more like His Son, Jesus Christ. The center of God's will is not a destination; it's a process. And that process begins this week and continues into next month and next year and five years from today—and for the rest of your life. Ask yourself,

What is His will for me in the next month?
In the next year?
Five years from now?

As long as you are walking with God and living His way, you are not likely to get off the path. And if by chance you do, He will get you right back on it. That's because you've been listening to God's voice. You will feel in your heart when you violate one of His directions.

Until we are living in the will of God, we are destined to have lives that are unfulfilled and incomplete. Knowing that God has a plan for you gives your life purpose as nothing else can. It simplifies everything because you don't have to figure it all out and make it all happen. You just have to look to the Lord, knowing He has it all figured out and He will make it happen.

Pray the Scriptures

Father, I want to know your will for my life. I belong to You, and I want to live in a way that pleases You. Your Word says, "that you will guide me continually" (Isaiah 58:11). I pray You will show me how to move forward in every area of my life. Lord, I pray there will be nothing in my life that dishonors You. If I am on the wrong path, I pray You will redirect my steps. I ask that You give me wisdom, guidance, and clear direction.

Look over the scriptures you studied today and let them guide you as you write your own prayer below that addresses your specific needs.

A PRAYER TO
Know Christ as Your Savior

The greatest decision you will ever make is whether or not you will follow Christ as your Lord and Savior. No choice has a bigger impact, and it's a decision every human being will make. Why? Because everyone carries guilt from past mistakes. Sometimes it's for things we know we've done; sometimes it's deep regret over what we fear we could have prevented; and sometimes it's for violation of certain natural laws we're not even aware of violating. Romans 3:23 says, "For all have sinned and fall short of the glory of God."

Whatever your past looks like, the load of guilt sits on us with crushing weight, and unless it's eliminated, it separates us from fellowship with God. But the good news is that God has given us a path to be reconciled to Him.

Key Scripture

"For whoever calls on the name of the LORD shall be saved" (Romans 10:13).

Prepare to Pray

You are never born again by chance. When you receive Jesus, it is because God the Father is drawing you in. Jesus said, "No one can come to Me unless the Father who sent Me draws him" (John 6:44). Once God draws you in, it's done—once and for all. You are released from guilt, your future is secure, and you are saved from death in every part of your life. Christianity is a living relationship with God through Jesus, His Son.

Salvation is not just something Jesus did for us; it is Jesus living in us. You may have been born into a Christian family or have attended a Christian church all your life, but if you haven't told God that you want to receive Jesus, you haven't been born into the kingdom of God. You can't inherit it, get it by osmosis, transplant it, implant it—or wish upon a star for it. You have to declare your faith before the Lord.

When you trust Christ as Lord and Savior of your life, you'll experience peace in knowing that your sins are forgiven and your future is secure. And not only is your eternal future secure—Jesus said anyone who believes in Him will have everlasting life (John 6:40)—but your future in this life is also secure. God promises that if we acknowledge Him, He will guide us safely where we need to go (Proverbs 3:6). This doesn't mean that we will instantly have all of our problems solved and never again know pain, but we will have the power within us to reach our full potential. We can never find any greater security than that.

Study the Scriptures

- Look up John 14:6 in your Bible. According to this passage, what role does Jesus play in being reconciled to God the Father?

- How would you explain what Jesus is saying in John 14:6 to a friend?

- At this point, how would you describe your relationship with Jesus? Have you trusted Him as your Lord and Savior? If not, what's holding you back?

- Read Acts 4:12 in your Bible. You've probably heard the saying, "There are many paths to God." Based on Acts 4:12, why is that statement untrue?

❁ **Look up the following passages and consider how they relate to trusting Christ as your Savior. How can you apply these truths to your own life?**

John 3:16	
Acts 2:21	
Romans 1:16	
Romans 5:1–5	

Respond to God's Word

When Jesus died on the cross, He also rose from the dead to break the power of death over anyone who receives His life. Jesus conquered death—whether at the end of our lives or in the multiple ways that we face death daily. In the death of our dreams, finances, health, or relationships, Jesus can bring His life to resurrect those dead places in us. Therefore we don't have to feel hopeless.

Jesus also gives to everyone who opens up to Him a quality of life that is meaningful, abundant, and fulfilling. He transcends our every limitation and boundary and enables us to do things we never would have been capable of aside from Him. He is the only one with power and authority over the emotions or bondage that torture us. He is the only one who can give us life

before death as well as life hereafter. Without Him we die a little every day. With Him we become more and more alive. If you haven't already trusted Christ as Your Savior now is the time!

Pray the Scriptures

Jesus, I believe You are the Son of God as You say You are. Although it's hard to comprehend love so great, I believe You laid down Your life for me so that I might have life eternally and abundantly now (John 3:16). I confess I have sinned against you and others (Romans 2:23). I ask You to forgive me for not living Your way (1 John 1:9). I need You to help me become all You created me to be. Come into my life and fill me with Your Holy Spirit. Let all the death in me be crowded out by the power of Your presence, and this day turn my life into a new beginning.

Look over the scriptures you studied today and let them guide you as you write your own prayer below that addresses your specific needs.

A PRAYER TO

Relate to God as Your Heavenly Father

One of the greatest blessings of being a Christian is having a heavenly Father who loves and cares for you. But acknowledging God as heavenly Father is sometimes difficult for people, especially if they didn't have a father or have been mistreated by a male parent or authority figure. One young woman told me, "Don't talk to me about God being a father. My father forced me to have sex with him until I left home, and now I'm unable to have a normal relationship with any man at all." Another confided to me, "My father beat me every time he came home drunk, and now I hate him. How can I think of God as a father?" A middle-aged man said, "My father never did anything for me. He was a weakling. He contributed nothing to my life and then eventually deserted us. Don't mention the word *father*."

Your life experiences may cause you to feel as these people did. But let me assure you that God will never be a father who comes home drunk, beats you, molests you, lies to you, betrays you, deserts you, or is too busy for you. He is different. He is a father who "knows the things you have need of" (Matthew 6:8) and will "give good things to those who ask Him" (Matthew 7:11). He will never leave nor forsake you, He will unfailingly have your best interest in mind, and He will always have more for you than you ever dreamed of for yourself.

Key Scriptures

"For you did not receive the spirit of bondage again to fear, but you received the Spirit of adoption by whom we cry out, 'Abba, Father.' The Spirit Himself bears witness with our spirit that we are children of God, and if children, then heirs—heirs of God and joint heirs with Christ, if indeed we suffer with Him, that we may also be glorified together" (Romans 8:15–17).

Prepare to Pray

Examine your relationship with the heavenly Father and see if any of the following statements apply to you:

- "I doubt that I am a beloved son or daughter to my heavenly Father."
- "I feel distant from Him."
- "I am afraid of Him."
- "I am angry with Him."
- "I feel abandoned by Him."
- "The thought of my heavenly Father brings tears of pain rather than joy."

If any one of these statements applies to you, you need a greater understanding of your heavenly Father's love for you. Ask Him for a deeper and more accurate understanding of His love for you. And then determine that you will not close yourself off from the Father who loves you. Give Him a chance to prove Himself faithful and show His power in your behalf.

When I was a new believer, I was strongly aware of God's love, especially His love for other people, but I didn't believe that He loved me as much as He loved them. The enormity of residual hurt and unforgiveness from the past, along with guilt, sadness, and fear, all served as a giant barrier that kept me from feeling His love. Because of these things, acknowledging God as Father took a great step of faith.

Study the Scriptures

- Read John 1:12–13. Based on this passage, what right did the Father give all people who trust Jesus as their Savior?

- What does it mean to you to be called "a child of God"?

- Read Romans 8:15–17. The apostle Paul used the term "Abba," which is a word a child would use when communicating with his or her father. What characteristics do you most cherish in a loving father?

- Think about the areas in your life where you need a loving, trustworthy, and faithful father. Practically speaking, how do you think your heavenly Father can meet those needs?

❁ **Look up the following passages and consider how they relate to knowing God as your heavenly Father. How can you apply these truths to your own life?**

Psalm 103:13	
Isaiah 63:16	
Luke 12:32	
2 Corinthians 6:18	

Respond to God's Word

It's one thing to know Jesus; it's another to know the Father. Salvation's purpose is not only to get us to Christ, but also to get us to the Father, where we understand our relationship with our Creator. We may have distorted images of Him because of everything that has happened to us, but we will not be able to see who we really are until we are able to see God as He really is. Then, out of the context of a relationship that secures and satisfies us, we can begin to grow. There is much healing ahead for us when we do. If you want to begin this process, or to renew your relationship with your heavenly Father, the following prayer will help you get started.

Pray the Scriptures

God, I acknowledge You as my heavenly Father today. I thank You that because of Jesus I have the right to be called a child of God (John 1:12). Heal any misconception I have of You. Where my earthly father has failed me and I have blamed You, forgive me and take away that hurt (1 John 1:9). Help me to remember that You are loving and compassionate (Psalm 103:13). I long to receive the inheritance that You have promised Your children (Romans 8:17).

Look over the scriptures you studied today and let them guide you as you write your own prayer below that addresses your specific needs.

A PRAYER TO
Know God as the Holy Spirit

The Christian life is impossible to live apart from God's power in our lives. Thankfully, God never intended for believers to attempt it apart from Him. Just before going to the cross, Jesus told His disciples that He would send a Helper (John 14:26). When I first heard the names *Helper* and *Comforter* in reference to the Holy Spirit, I knew immediately I wanted those attributes of God in my life. But I first had to acknowledge the Holy Spirit's existence and then be open to His working in me.

A common trap that believers often fall into is ignoring the Holy Spirit's presence. Although it's never intentional, how often do we go about the Christian life pretending we can do it on our own? And then we wind up worn out and frustrated and wondering why we aren't making more progress. The truth is, it's impossible to live the life God intends for us to live without active dependence on the Holy Spirit.

Key Scriptures

"In Him you also trusted, after you heard the word of truth, the gospel of your salvation; in whom also, having believed, you were sealed with the Holy Spirit of promise, who is the guarantee of our inheritance until the redemption of the purchased possession, to the praise of His glory" (Ephesians 1:13–14).

Prepare to Pray

The Holy Spirit is the Spirit of God sent by Jesus to give us comfort, to build us up, to guide us in all truth, to bring us spiritual gifts, to help us pray more effectively, to give us wisdom and revelation, and to help us know God's will for our lives.

It's foolish to pretend the Holy Spirit doesn't exist or say that Jesus didn't mean it when He promised He would send the Holy Spirit to us, or suggest that God was just kidding when He said He was pouring out His Spirit on all humankind. The Holy Spirit is not a vapor or a mystical cloud; He is the third person of the Trinity.

I have discovered over the years, however, that the infilling of the Holy Spirit is ongoing and ever deepening. We have to be willing to open up to each new level and dimension so that He can enable us to accomplish what we could never do without this full measure of His love, power, and life.

Study the Scriptures

- Read John 14:15–18. Write down four to five things these verses say about the Holy Spirit.

- **Read John 16:7–15. Just before going to the cross, Jesus provided His disciples with more details about the Holy Spirit. What new information did Jesus provide?**

- **Based on the information found in these passages, in what specific ways do you see the Holy Spirit at work in your life?**

- **Look up 1 Corinthians 12:3. According to this passage, what role does the Holy Spirit play in acknowledging Jesus as Lord?**

❁ **Look up the following passages and consider how they relate to knowing God as the Holy Spirit. How can you apply these truths to your own life?**

John 14:16–17	
Luke 11:13	
John 16:13	
Acts 2:38–39	

Respond to God's Word

You might be wondering, *How can I know if the Holy Spirit is working in my life?* If your lips can say, "Jesus is Lord," you can be sure the Spirit of God is working in your life already. The Bible says, "I will put My Spirit within you and cause you to walk in My statutes, and you will keep My judgments and do them" (Ezekiel 36:27). The Holy Spirit works the wholeness of God into us. And there need be no fear or concern about this, because we alone of God's creation have a special place built in us where His Spirit can reside. That place will always be empty until it is filled with Him.

We don't want to have "a form of godliness" but deny "its power" (2 Timothy 3:5); denying God's power limits what God can do in our lives and prevents us from moving into all God has for us. Nor do we want to be "always learning and never able to come to the knowledge of the truth" (2 Timothy 3:7). Unless the Holy Spirit coaches us from within, our knowledge of the truth will always be limited, and our spiritual health will be incomplete. Don't limit what God can do in you by failing to acknowledge His Holy Spirit in your life.

Pray the Scriptures

God, help me understand all I need to know about You and the workings of Your Spirit in my life. Fill me with Your Holy Spirit in a fresh new way this day and work powerfully in me. I pray the Holy Spirit will be my greatest influence. Help me be sensitive to anything that is unpleasing to You or any behavior that might quench the Spirit's work in me (1 Thessalonians 5:19). Make me quick to repent of sin (John 16:8). Teach me Your truth and remind me of Your promises (John 16:13). Empower me to walk in the power of the Holy Spirit and glorify Jesus in every area of my life (John 16:14).

Look over the scriptures you studied today and let them guide you as you write your own prayer below that addresses your specific needs.

A PRAYER TO
Know God as Lord Over Every Area of Your Life

Early in my walk with Christ, I found I needed to expose many areas of my life to His influence. This was difficult because it called for my deepening trust. Until then I'd had few positive experiences when someone other than myself was in control of my life. In every house I lived in when I was growing up, we always had rooms that no one was allowed to see. They contained a confusing clutter of items rendered useless by their overwhelming number and lack of order. One reason my mother never wanted anyone to come to our house (aside from the fact that it was too exhausting for her to keep up a front of normalcy) was that she was afraid someone would see the secret rooms. These rooms were reflective of our family life. The secret of my mother's mental illness had to be hidden at all costs.

When I grew up, it was as if those secret rooms in our home became secret places in my heart. I kept so many parts of me hidden that I lived in terror that they would be discovered and I'd be rejected. When I first received Jesus into my heart, I showed Him into the guest room. The problem was, He wasn't content to stay there. He kept knocking on one door after another until I was opening doors to rooms I had never even known were there. He exposed every dark corner of each room to His cleansing light. I soon realized that He wanted me to acknowledge Him as Lord over every area of my life.

Key Scripture

"Behold, I stand at the door and knock. If anyone hears My voice and opens the door, I will come in to him and dine with him, and he with Me" (Revelation 3:20).

Prepare to Pray

When you invite Jesus into the home of your being (when you are born again), you are supposed to also give Him the run of the house—making Him Lord over your life. However, many of us are slow to do that completely. Whether we admit it or not, we hesitate to believe that God can be trusted with every area of our lives. The Bible says,

> Trust in the LORD with *all* your heart,
> And lean not on your own understanding;
> In *all* your ways acknowledge Him,
> And He shall direct your paths. (Proverbs 3:5–6, emphasis added)

Notice that word *all.* It's very specific. If we want things to work out well, we have to acknowledge Him as Lord over all areas of our lives. I had to be willing to give God the right-of-way by frequently saying, "Jesus, be Lord over every area of my life." Then as He pointed to places where I had not opened the door to His rulership, I let Him in. I know now that God does this with all people who invite Him to dwell in their lives. Some people give Him total access to the home of their being right away. Others leave Him standing in the entryway indefinitely. Many people do as I did and allow Him to gain entrance slowly.

When He knocks on different doors inside you, just know that He will never bulldoze His way in and break down the walls. He will simply knock persistently and quietly and, as He's invited, will come to gently occupy each corner of your life to clean and rebuild.

Study the Scriptures

- Look up and read Psalm 103 and as you read pay special attention to what the psalmist reveals about God's character. Write down several characteristics that stand out.

- How does the psalmist's description of God influence how you feel about letting Him into "every room" and acknowledging Him as Lord over every area of your life?

- Glance back at Psalm 103:14 and note that the psalmist says that "He remembers that we are dust." Why is it significant that God understands our fragility?

- Are there areas you are holding back from God? If so, what's keeping you from submitting your whole self to Him?

- Look up the following passages and consider how they relate to knowing God as Lord over every area of your life. How can you apply these truths to your own life?

Exodus 20:3	
Mark 12:30	
Philippians 2:10–11	
1 Peter 5:6–7	

Respond to God's Word

In Jesus' time on earth, He touched dead bodies and restored them to life. He also touched lepers and restored them to health. He will do as much for you right now. He will never say, "You are untouchable to Me; you are too far gone; you smell too bad; your failure is too great; your circumstances are too dead."

If something has died in you or your life, God is moved by compassion for it. Wherever there are dead places in you, He will breathe life into them. He cares about your feelings and weaknesses. He desires to touch you with healing and life, but He will not do it unless you first acknowledge Him as Lord over those areas and invite Him into the situation. The fact that He won't touch those areas without an invitation from you is not an indication that He doesn't care; rather, He has given you a choice. Will you choose to open up and share every part of yourself with Him and let Him reign in your life?

When the barriers are down, He is not restricted from going into any area He desires. That means we are open to whatever God wants to do in us, no matter how uncomfortable it may feel at the time. The happiest people I know put all of their lives into God's hands, knowing that wherever He is enthroned, no threat of hell can succeed against them.

Pray the Scriptures

God, I acknowledge You as Lord over every area of my life this day. I give You all of me. Help me walk in Your perfect will in all that I do and everything that I say (Proverbs 3:5–6). I praise You for being trustworthy. I ask You to redeem my life from the pit and crown me with faithful love and compassion. I pray You will satisfy me with good things (Psalm 103:4–5). Lord, I thank You that You haven't dealt with me as my sins deserve, but instead You have shown me great mercy (Psalm 103:10).

Look over the scriptures you studied today and let them guide you as you write your own prayer below that addresses your specific needs.

A PRAYER TO

Know God as the Name That Meets Your Every Need

The Lord has many names in the Bible, and each one expresses an aspect of His nature or one of His attributes. When we acknowledge Him by those names, we invite Him to be those things to us. One of the reasons we do not have the wholeness, fulfillment, and peace we desire is that we have not acknowledged God as the answer to our every need.

We think, *He may have given me eternal life, but I don't know if He can handle my financial problems.* Or we think, *I know He can lead me to a better job, but I'm not sure if He can mend this marriage.* Or, *He healed my back, but I don't know if He can take away my depression.* The truth is, He is everything we need, and we have to remember that always. In fact, it's good to tell yourself daily, "God is everything I need," and then say the name of the Lord that answers your specific need at that moment.

- Do you need hope? He is called our Hope. Pray, "Jesus, You are my Hope."
- Are you weak? He is called our Strength. Pray, "Jesus, You are my Strength."
- Do you need advice? He is called Counselor. Pray, "Jesus, You are my Counselor."
- Do you feel oppressed? He is called Deliverer. Pray, "Jesus, You are my Deliverer."
- Are you lonely? He is called Companion and Friend. Pray, "Jesus, You are my Companion and Friend."

Key Scripture

"The name of the LORD is a strong tower;
The righteous run to it and are safe" (Proverbs 18:10).

Prepare to Pray

Below are thirty of the biblical names of the Lord. Read this list over, keeping in mind that God desires to be all these things to you. Every day you can choose at least one name that is applicable to your needs and frequently thank God that He is that for you. Acknowledging that He is these things is the first step toward the realization of His becoming them in your life. Keep in mind that everything about His personality is stronger than anything negative in yours.

Thirty Attributes of Jesus

1. He is my Restorer (Psalm 23:3).
2. He is my Helper (John 14:16).
3. He is my Strength (Isaiah 12:2).
4. He is my Redeemer (Isaiah 59:20).
5. He is my Hope (Psalm 71:5).
6. He is my Patience (Romans 15:5).
7. He is my Truth (John 14:6).
8. He is my Resting Place (Jeremiah 50:6).
9. He is my Overcomer (John 16:33).
10. He is my Light (John 8:12).

11. He is the Power of God (1 Corinthians 1:24).
12. He is my Bread of Life (John 6:35).
13. He is my Fortress (Psalm 18:2).
14. He is my Refuge from the Storm (Isaiah 25:4).
15. He is my Everlasting Father (Isaiah 9:6).
16. He is the Author of My Faith (Hebrews 12:2).
17. He is my Deliverer (Psalm 70:5).
18. He is my Counselor (Psalm 16:7).
19. He is my Peace (Ephesians 2:14).
20. He is my Rewarder (Hebrews 11:6).
21. He is my Healer (Malachi 4:2).
22. He is my Shield (Psalm 33:20).
23. He is my Wisdom of God (1 Corinthians 1:24).
24. He is my Purifier (Malachi 3:3).
25. He is my Hiding Place (Psalm 32:7).
26. He is my Shade from the Heat (Isaiah 25:4).
27. He is my Refiner (Malachi 3:2–3).
28. He is my Resurrection (John 11:25).
29. He is the Lifter of My Head (Psalm 3:3).
30. He is my Stronghold in the Day of Trouble (Nahum 1:7).

Study the Scriptures

- Read Matthew 1:23. What does "Immanuel" mean?

- Why is it significant that Jesus is present and with us?

- Glance back at the list of thirty attributes of Jesus. Which ones most resonate with you in this season of life?

- How can the list of Jesus' attributes guide your prayer life? Which names do you need to include in your prayers?

- Look up the following passages and consider how they relate to knowing God as the name who meets every need. How can you apply these truths to your own life?

Psalm 20:7	
Psalm 124:8	
Romans 10:13	
Philippians 2:9–10	
Hebrews 13:5–6	

Respond to God's Word

Are you quick to acknowledge Jesus' lordship in your life? Certain guarantees and rewards are inherent in simply acknowledging the name of Jesus. For example, the Bible says, "The name of the LORD is a strong tower; the righteous run to it and are safe" (Proverbs 18:10). There is a covering of protection over anyone who turns to the name of the Lord. The Bible says that if we acknowledge the name of the Lord, He will acknowledge us. And there is an intimacy that grows as long as this acknowledgment is sustained.

Pray the Scriptures

Jesus, thank You that You are Immanuel, God with us. Thank You that You are with me and You are everything I need. Jesus, Your Word says You are Truth. Guide me in Your truth (John 14:6). You are the Source of all wisdom, and I pray You will give me wisdom in all my circumstances (1 Corinthians 1:24). Father, You are the Author of my faith—and I pray You will increase my faith and empower me to walk the path You have for me (Hebrews 12:2). Please help me sense Your presence in a new way today.

Look over the scriptures you studied today and let them guide you as you write your own prayer below that addresses your specific needs.

A PRAYER TO
Mature in Your Faith

When I first became a Christian, I thought that after you received Jesus into your life, that was it. Becoming a Christian meant you'd made it—and there would be no more problems. It didn't take me long to realize that isn't the case. I had trusted Christ as my Savior, and my salvation guaranteed I would spend eternity with Christ in heaven. But my life here on earth still needed work. I had to do certain things to sustain life and become spiritually and emotionally healthy. What a revelation!

I had pursued physical fitness and proper body care for many years, and so I quickly related to this discipline—doing something good for yourself, no matter how much you didn't feel like doing it, so that you would be able to enjoy good health and well-being. I began to understand that just as the physical body needs to be fed, exercised, and cleansed, so the spirit and soul need replenishing. I learned about five key elements—spiritual practices—that will strengthen our relationship with God:

1. The Word of God
2. Prayer
3. Praise
4. Confession
5. Ongoing forgiveness

Key Scripture

"Be diligent to present yourself approved to God, a worker who does not need to be ashamed, rightly dividing the word of truth" (2 Timothy 2:15).

Prepare to Pray

If we neglect spiritual practices like Bible reading, prayer, confession, and asking for God's forgiveness, we end up with cracks in our foundation. When we have cracks in our foundation, we never end up where we are supposed to be and we can never fully know God's will. Some people do "get by," never doing any of these things, but as a new Christian, I wasn't interested in getting by. I'd been doing that for years. I wanted true spiritual well-being and a sense of purpose and direction. I wanted God's will for my life—and I wanted to experience a close relationship with God.

Keep in mind, we don't engage in spiritual practices to "earn points" or favor with God. If you have trusted Christ as your Savior, you already have God's favor. We engage in spiritual practices because they put us in a posture to grow in our faith and receive God's grace. There's nothing in this world that will improve your life more than a close relationship with God. And it is through these spiritual practices that we draw near to God. James 4:8 says, "Draw near to God and He will draw near to you."

Spiritual practices give us the opportunity to spend time in God's presence, learn from His Word, and talk to Him in prayer. It's through committing ourselves to these practices that we mature in our faith. Will it take some effort? Yes, it absolutely will. Good relationships, good health, and being good at what you do all require some sacrifice, discipline, discomfort, and even some pain. Spiritual wholeness is like that too.

Study the Scriptures

- Look up and read 1 Corinthians 3:1–3. Why did the apostle Paul refer to some as "babes or infants in Christ"? What does that description suggest?

- Glance back at verse 3. What are some of the characteristics of immature believers that Paul lists?

- How would you describe a spiritually mature believer in Christ?

- All believers have room for spiritual growth. Can you name some specific ways you'd like to grow and mature in your faith?

❁ **Look up the following passages and consider how they relate to maturing in your faith. How can you apply these truths to your own life?**

Proverbs 10:25	
Matthew 7:24–25	
Romans 10:17	
2 Timothy 2:19–20	

Respond to God's Word

Spiritual practices are meant to be practiced both alone and in a group setting. It's important to set aside a regular time to be alone with God when you can read your Bible, pray, confess your sins, and simply spend time in God's presence. But it's also important to be an active member of a biblical community. The book of Acts describes the earliest Christians this way: "And they continued steadfastly in the apostles' doctrine and fellowship, in the breaking of bread, and in prayers" (Acts 2:42).

It's important to study God's Word with other believers, to share conversation over meals, and have people who will pray with you and for you. Also, it's crucial to spend time with believers who are more mature in their faith, because you'll learn from them. And as you grow in your faith, it will be your turn to mentor younger believers or serve in whatever way God calls you to.

Pray the Scriptures

Lord, help me remember the importance of Your Word, prayer, praise, confession, and ongoing forgiveness in my daily walk. Help me not neglect any one of them. Open my mind and heart to walk even deeper with You in each of these areas. Your Word says that if I draw near to You, You will draw near to me (James 4:8). Lord, give me the desire, discipline, and grace to draw near to You with everything I've got. I pray I will mature in faith and be counted among those who have no need to be ashamed, but that I will have a mature understanding of You and Your Word (2 Timothy 2:15).

Look over the scriptures you studied today and let them guide you as you write your own prayer below that addresses your specific needs.

A PRAYER FOR
A Solid Foundation in God's Truth

Early on in my life as a believer I recall my pastor encouraging us to read the Word of God. I thought, *First Pastor asks us to bring our own Bibles; now he wants us to read them ourselves?* I had purchased a Bible in a translation that I could understand, just as he had requested, but I thought that he would teach us from it and we would follow along.

I had given up trying to read the Bible years before when several unsuccessful attempts brought discouragement and frustration. I found the writing so foreign, I couldn't understand it at all. But my pastor taught from the Scriptures with amazing clarity, and I hung on every word. It was like watching a movie so reflective of my own life that I became involved in the action. *Could it be,* I asked myself, *that I might feel that same way when I read the Bible at home alone?*

Key Scripture

"All Scripture is given by inspiration of God, and is profitable for doctrine, for reproof, for correction, for instruction in righteousness, that the man of God may be complete, thoroughly equipped for every good work"
(2 Timothy 3:16–17).

Prepare to Pray

Gradually the Bible became God's voice in my ear. When I heard certain old, familiar words in my mind, such as *You're worthless. You'll never amount to anything. Why try?* I also heard the words of God saying, *You are fearfully and wonderfully made. I will lift you up from the gates of death. You will be blessed if you put your trust in Me* (Psalm 139:14; 9:13; 2:12).

The more I read, the more I saw that God's laws were good. They were there for my benefit, and I could trust them. It became clear to me that conscience wasn't an adequate indicator of right or wrong. I could see that things can really only be found right or wrong in the light of God's Word. Such guidelines, rather than restricting, were actually liberating to me.

Study the Scriptures

- Look up and read Matthew 4:4. In your own words, describe what you think Jesus was communicating in this passage.

- In this season of life, how would you describe your Bible reading habits?

- Look up and read Hebrews 4:12. How does this passage describe God's Word?

- Practically speaking, what small changes do you need to make to set aside a consistent time to read God's Word?

- Look up the following passages and consider how they relate to having a solid foundation in God's truth. How can you apply these truths to your own life?

Isaiah 40:8	
Psalm 19:7–8	
Psalm 107:20	
Psalm 119:105	
John 15:7	

Respond to God's Word

You may be thinking, *I can't afford the time it takes to read the Bible every day.* Let me challenge you to reconsider. I have listed fifteen reasons to read the Bible daily. After you read this list, you will realize that we can't afford to let a day go by without absorbing at least a few verses of the Word into our hearts and minds.

Fifteen Reasons to Read the Bible Daily

1. To be rid of anxiety and have peace (Psalm 119:165)
2. To set things right when life is out of control (Psalm 19:7–8)
3. To have direction and know God's will (Psalm 119:105)
4. To experience healing and deliverance (Psalm 107:20)
5. To grow in the Lord (1 Peter 2:2)
6. To have strength, comfort, and hope (Psalm 119:28, 50, 114)
7. To shape yourself and your life correctly (Psalm 119:11)
8. To be able to see clearly (Psalm 119:130)
9. To know what's really in your heart (Hebrews 4:12)
10. To build faith (Romans 10:17)
11. To have joy (Psalm 16:11)
12. To understand God's power (John 1:3)
13. To have more life in this life (Psalm 119:50)
14. To distinguish good from evil (Psalm 119:101–102)
15. To understand God's love for you (John 1:14)

Pray the Scriptures

Lord, I thank You for Your Word. Reveal Yourself to me as I read it and let it come alive in my heart and mind. Show me what I need to know. Let Your Word penetrate anything that would block me from receiving all You want to say to me today. I pray Your Word will be alive and active in me (Hebrews 4:12). Father, I ask that Your Word penetrate down to every fiber of my being—down to my bones and marrow. Jesus, I pray Your Word will be a lamp to my feet and light to my path (Psalm 119:105).

Look over the scriptures you studied today and let them guide you as you write your own prayer below that addresses your specific needs.

A PRAYER TO
Know the Power of Prayer

If you keep a prayer journal there's a good chance you've recorded prayer requests that ask for things like: getting a job, healing from a sickness, and providing for a specific need. Of course, we're wise to ask for those types of things and the Bible invites us to "cast all of our cares on him" (1 Peter 5:7).

But prayer is not just asking for things—although that certainly is part of it. Far more important, prayer is talking with God. It's getting close to and spending time with the One you love. It's seeking Him first, getting to know Him better, being with Him, and waiting in His presence. It's acknowledging Him as the source of power upon whom you depend. It's taking the time to say, "Speak to my heart, Lord, and tell me what I need to hear."

Key Scripture

"For your Father knows the things you have need of before you ask Him" (Matthew 6:8).

Prepare to Pray

You might be wondering, *If God already knows what I need, why do I even need to ask for anything?* As a new believer, I asked my pastor the same question. In his usual clear manner, he explained, "Because God has given us a free will. He has set it up so that we always have a choice about everything we do, including whether or not we choose to communicate with Him. He will never intervene where man does not want Him."

Of course! I thought. God wants us to desire to be with Him. There is no love relationship if one person has to dictate how the other must think, feel, and act. "God knows our thoughts," my pastor continued, "but He responds to our prayers. We have to come to a place of realizing that prayer is a privilege that is always ours, but the power in prayer is always His. Without God, we can't do it. Without us, God won't do it."

That put a whole new perspective on the subject. Things wouldn't happen in my life unless I prayed. And I was no longer just asking for things; I was partnering with God. I was aligning my spirit with His, and together we would see that His perfect will would be done.

Study the Scriptures

- Look up and read Colossians 4:2. What three things does this passage instruct believers to do in their prayer life?

- How would you describe your prayer life in this season of your life? In what areas would you like to improve?

- Glance back at Colossians 4:2. Notice how the apostle Paul instructs believers to "continue earnestly," or some translations say, "devote yourselves" to prayer. Write down two or three ways you could make it a point to pray throughout the day.

- Paul lists "giving thanks" as an important aspect of prayer. Write down two or three things you are grateful to God for and include those things in your prayer time.

- Look up the following passages and consider how they relate to knowing the power of prayer in Jesus's name. How can you apply these truths to your own life?

Psalm 95:2–3	
Luke 11:1–2	

John 15:7–8	
1 Peter 3:12	

Respond to God's Word

We all know that when friends don't see each other and communicate frequently, they can become emotionally separated. Well, it's the same with you and God. If you don't keep in touch with Him, you begin to feel distant from Him even when you're not. This is why you must pray daily. Also, when you spend time with someone you respect, the character of that person rubs off on you. When you are in the presence of God, His character is formed in you.

Many of us are especially vulnerable to the Enemy's attack on our self-worth. It doesn't take much to discourage us, and feeling distant from God will do it. That's why it's important to start the day with some kind of prayer. We have to establish ourselves and our lives as being connected to Him. We can't receive God's best for our lives, and we can't push back the things that were never God's will for us, except through prayer. We have to learn that we can't leave our lives to chance. We have to pray over anything that concerns us, no matter how big—"With God nothing will be impossible" (Luke 1:37)—or how small—"The very hairs of your head are all numbered" (Matthew 10:30). If you have any doubt about the importance of prayer or if you are still praying on an on-again, off-again basis, go through the fifteen reasons to pray below. I find that reading the Scripture passages that support them is very motivational too.

Fifteen Reasons to Pray

1. To seek the face of the Lord and know Him better (Psalm 27:8)
2. To get your eyes off your problems and onto the Lord (Psalm 121:1)
3. To speak to God (1 Peter 3:12)
4. To unburden your heart (Psalm 142:1–2)
5. To make your requests known to God (Matthew 21:22)
6. To hear God (Proverbs 8:34)
7. To be free of suffering (James 5:13)
8. To resist temptation (Matthew 26:41)
9. To be rescued from distress (Psalm 107:19)
10. To receive God's reward (Matthew 6:6)
11. To withstand evil (Ephesians 6:13)
12. To have joy (John 16:24)
13. To get close to God (Isaiah 64:7)
14. To be healed emotionally (James 5:13)
15. To have peace (Philippians 4:6–7)

Pray the Scriptures

Father, I pray You will help me to develop a powerful prayer life. I ask You to give me the motivation and discipline to devote myself to prayer, help me to continue earnestly in prayer, to be vigilant, and to be a woman who is quick to offer thanksgiving for the many ways You bless me (Colossians 4:2). Lord, I thank You that You invite me to pray and cast all my cares on You (1 Peter 5:7). But Lord, I pray I won't only seek Your hand of blessing, but that I will also seek Your face (2 Chronicles 7:14).

Look over the scriptures you studied today and let them guide you as you write your own prayer below that addresses your specific needs.

A PRAYER TO

Understand the Freedom of Praise

Worship is powerful because God's presence comes to dwell in our midst when we praise Him, and in His presence, we find healing, transformation, and direction for our lives. In fact, the more time we spend praising the Lord, the more we will see ourselves and our circumstances grow in wholeness and completeness. That's because praise softens our hearts and makes them pliable. It also covers us protectively. The more the pliability and covering are maintained, the more quickly our hearts can be molded and healed.

Please read the preceding paragraph again. Underline it, circle it, draw arrows pointing to it, commit it to memory, write it on your hand, or do whatever you have to do to remember it. This important truth is the first thing we forget and the last thing we remember because our flesh doesn't naturally want to do it. Praise and worship of God are always acts of will. Sometimes our problems or the burdens we carry choke out our good intentions, so we have to make the effort to establish praise as a way of life. And it becomes a way of life when we make it our first reaction to what we face and not a last resort. That's when we find true freedom in the Lord.

Key Scripture

"Therefore by Him let us continually offer the sacrifice of praise to God, that is, the fruit of our lips, giving thanks to His name" (Hebrews 13:15).

Prepare to Pray

Now is the time to start being thankful to God for everything in your life. Thank Him for His Word, His faithfulness, His love, His grace, His healing. Thank Him for what He has done for you personally. If you have trouble thinking of something, then thank Him that you're still breathing and that you can read. Keep in mind that whatever you thank the Lord for—peace, financial blessing, health, a new job, an end to depression—will start the process of its being released to you at that time.

In the Old Testament, the people who carried the ark of the covenant stopped every six steps to worship. We, too, need to remind ourselves not to go very far without stopping to worship. For spiritual well-being, we have to be six-step persons and continually invite the presence of the Lord to rule in our situations. We have to be free to praise Him no matter what our circumstances.

Study the Scriptures

- Look up and read Psalm 34:1. Notice how the Psalmist says, "I will bless the LORD at all times." What are some practical ways you can build praise into your lifestyle?

- Does praising God come easy for you or is it an area in which you struggle? Write down the current ways you praise and give thanks to God.

- If you are already in the habit of praising God, how does praise influence your frame of mind and outlook?

- Glance at the chart Fifteen Reasons to Praise God on the following page. What stands out to you on this list?

- Look up the following passages and consider how they relate to the freedom of praising God. How can you apply these truths to your own life?

Psalm 18:1–3	
Psalm 96:1–6	
Psalm 147:1	
Psalm 150:6	

Respond to God's Word

The reason people don't give thanks to God in praise is because they don't know Him well enough. The more you know of Him, the more you perceive His goodness, the more you can't help but thank, praise, and worship Him for who He is and what He has done. And the more you do that, the more joy you will have in your heart. Remember, praise and worship is an act of the will. There will be times when "you don't feel like" praising God. But if you push through the resistance, you'll find freedom on the other side.

Fifteen Reasons to Praise God

1. To enthrone God and acknowledge His greatness (Psalm 95:1–5)
2. To increase our awareness of God's presence (Psalm 103)
3. To have the joy of the Lord (Psalm 30)
4. To acknowledge God's hand in every area of our lives (Psalm 91)
5. To release God's power into our situations (Psalm 144)
6. To know God better (Psalm 50:23)
7. To break our chains of bondage and bring deliverance (Psalm 50:14–15)
8. To be under God's covering of safety and protection (Psalms 95:6–7)
9. To strengthen the soul and be transformed (Psalm 138:1–3)
10. To receive guidance and establish God's purposes in our lives (Psalm 16:7–11)
11. To thwart the devil's plans for our destruction (Psalm 92)
12. To dissipate doubt and increase faith (Psalm 27)
13. To be delivered from fear (Psalm 34)
14. To bring a fresh flow of His Holy Spirit in us (Psalm 40)
15. To possess all that God has promised for us (Psalm 147)

Pray the Scriptures

Father, You are worthy of all praise, worship, and glory (Psalm 95:1–5). I praise You, for You are the Creator of all things and the holy God of the universe. Father, the heavens declare Your glory (Psalm 19:1). I pray You will allow me to know You in increasing measure that I might praise You all the more. Help me to see Your majesty and holiness. I pray that I will always bless You and that Your praise will continually be in my mouth (Psalm 34:1). Give me eyes to see Your goodness and lips that are eager to worship Your glorious name. Jesus, You are the name that is above all names (Philippians 2:9). Help me to magnify You and understand that You are greater and more powerful than any problem or circumstance in my life.

Look over the scriptures you studied today and let them guide you as you write your own prayer below that addresses your specific needs.

A PRAYER TO
Quickly Confess Your Sins

Unconfessed sin affects our whole life. And often we don't recognize it. After I came to know the Lord and experienced that warm, close, rich feeling of walking with God, I still fell back into some old, familiar bad habits. I had only known the Lord for a few months before I went out on tour with a music group. None of them were believers, and so it was easy to be drawn back into their drinking and partying lifestyle. When I came home after a month of that decadent life, I went back to church but I didn't feel the intimacy with God that I had been experiencing before I left. I recognized that it was probably because God was not pleased with the way I had been living the past four weeks. I began to feel guilty, depressed, and hopeless about my life again.

The following Sunday, my pastor talked about the damage unconfessed sin can do to your soul. I knew that God was talking to me. Right there in church I quietly confessed to the Lord my sinful actions of the past month. The moment I did, I felt that wonderful sense of God's love again, and I couldn't stop the tears from flowing. Here I had been thinking that God had turned His back on me, but the truth was that my actions had separated me from Him. I hated that feeling of being distant from God, and I vowed to never let unconfessed sin come between me and the Lord again. I would try my best to live His way, but if I failed, I would confess it immediately so I could receive His forgiveness and not lose the close fellowship with Him that I had come to treasure so dearly.

Key Scripture

"If we confess our sins, He is faithful and just to forgive us our sins and to cleanse us from all unrighteousness" (1 John 1:9).

Prepare to Pray

When sin is unconfessed, it becomes a subtle growth, wrapping its tentacles around every part of our beings until we are paralyzed. The agony of it is accurately described in the Bible by King David:

> When I kept silent, my bones grew old
> Through my groaning all the day long.
> For day and night Your hand was heavy upon me;
> My vitality was turned into the drought of summer.
> I acknowledged my sin to You,
> And my iniquity I have not hidden.
> I said, "I will confess my transgressions to the LORD,"
> And You forgave the iniquity of my sin. (Psalm 32:3–5)

When sin is left unconfessed, a wall goes up between you and God. Even though the sin may have stopped, if it hasn't been confessed before the Lord, it will still weigh you down, dragging you back toward the past you are trying to leave behind and keeping you from moving into the future God has for you. I know because I used to carry around a bag of failures on my back that was so heavy I could barely move. I didn't realize how spiritually stooped over I had become. When I confessed my sins, I actually felt the weight being lifted.

Study the Scriptures

- Look up and read Psalm 51. This is a passage that King David wrote after a serious season of sin. What stands out to you in this passage?

- How would you describe David's tone in this passage?

- Notice in Psalm 51:12 David writes, "Restore to me the joy of Your salvation." How does sin impact our joy?

- Do you have sin that you need to confess to God? Using Psalm 51 as your model, spend a few moments confessing your sins to God.

❁ Look up the following passages and consider how they relate to quickly confessing your sins to God. How can you apply these truths to your own life?

Exodus 34:9	
Psalm 32:5	
John 16:8	
James 5:16	

Respond to God's Word

For confession to work, repentance must go along with it. *Repentance* literally means a change of mind. It means to turn your back, walk away, and decide not to do it again. It means getting your thinking aligned correctly with God. Because we are not perfect, confession and repentance are ongoing. There are always new levels of Jesus' life that need to be worked in us. We fall short of the glory of God in ways that we can't yet even imagine.

Always keep in mind that God's ways are for your benefit. Confession is not for Him to find out something; He already knows. Confession is for you to be made whole. He is not standing over you, waiting to punish you for what you do wrong. He doesn't have to, because the punishment is inherent in the sin. People who confess find mercy and God's unlimited power.

Pray the Scriptures

Father, Your Word says that if I confess my sins, You will be faithful to forgive me and cleanse me of all unrighteousness (1 John 1:9). I confess that I have sinned against You (list specific things). I ask for Your forgiveness in Jesus' name. I pray You will also forgive me of the sins that I am committing that I am not aware of. I pray You will cleanse me from secret faults (Psalm 19:12). I pray You will make me sensitive to the Holy Spirit's conviction and make me quick to confess and repent of my sins. Create in me a clean heart, O God, and renew a steadfast spirit within me (Psalm 51:10).

Look over the scriptures you studied today and let them guide you as you write your own prayer below that addresses your specific needs.

A PRAYER TO
Forgive Yourself, God, and Others

Forgiveness leads to life. Unforgiveness is a slow death. Not forgiving someone doesn't jeopardize your salvation and keep you out of heaven, but it does mean you won't enjoy all that God has for you. And you may find yourself wandering around outside the center of God's will. The first step to forgiving is to receive God's forgiveness and let its reality penetrate the deepest part of your being. When we realize how much we have been forgiven, it's easier to understand that we have no right to pass judgment on one another. Being forgiven and released from everything we've ever done wrong is such a miraculous gift, how could we refuse to obey God when He asks us to forgive others as He has forgiven us? Easy! We focus our thoughts on the person who has wronged us rather than on the God who makes all things right.

Forgiveness is a two-way street: God forgives you, and you forgive others. God forgives you quickly and completely upon your confession of wrongdoing. You are to forgive others quickly and completely, whether they admit failure or not. Most of the time people don't feel they've done anything wrong anyway, and if they do, they certainly don't want to admit it to you.

Key Scripture

"And forgive us our debts, as we forgive our debtors" (Matthew 6:12).

Prepare to Pray

Forgiveness is a choice that we make. We base our decision not on what we feel like doing but on what we know is right. Growing up, I suffered neglect and abuse from my mentally ill mother. As an adult, I did not feel like forgiving her. Instead, I chose to forgive her because God's Word says, "Forgive, and you will be forgiven" (Luke 6:37). That verse also says that we shouldn't judge if we don't want to be judged ourselves. I had to understand that God loves my mother as much as He loves me. He loves all people as much as He loves me. He loves the murderer, the rapist, the prostitute, and the thief. And He hates all of their sins as much as He hates ours. He hates murdering, raping, and stealing as much as He hates pride, gossiping, and unforgiveness. We may sit and compare our sins to other people's and say, "Mine aren't so bad," but God says they all stink, so we shouldn't worry about whose smell the worst. The most important thing to remember when it comes to forgiving is that forgiveness doesn't make the other person right; it makes you free.

Study the Scriptures

- Look up and read Luke 23:34. What did Jesus pray as He hung on the cross?

- Look up and read Romans 5:8. How would you explain this verse to a friend?

- How does Jesus set the example for believers and forgiveness?

- Most people struggle with forgiveness. Do you tend to struggle more with forgiving yourself or forgiving others? What role do you think prayer has in your ability to forgive?

- Look up the following passages and consider how they relate to forgiveness. How can you apply these truths to your own life?

Matthew 6:9–12	
Matthew 6:15	
Colossians 3:12–13	
Ephesians 4:32	

Respond to God's Word

While forgiving others is crucial, forgiveness is also needed in two other areas. One area is forgiving yourself. So many of us think, *I should be achieving this; I should be this kind of person; I should have done more than I have by this time in my life.* I certainly was burdened by these kinds of thoughts. God is the only One who is perfect. We have to be able to say, "Self, I forgive you for not being perfect, and I thank You, God, that You are right now making me into all that You created me to be."

Some of us have to forgive ourselves for the mistakes we have made. Before I came to know the Lord, I wasted my life doing drugs, dabbling in the occult, and getting involved in unhealthy relationships. When I was finally able to forgive myself, I realized that God could use even those experiences for His glory. I am now able to speak into the lives of women who have committed these same errors. They see that what God has helped me to overcome is possible for them too.

Besides forgiving others and yourself, you must also check to see if you need to forgive God. If you've been mad at Him, say so. You won't crush God's ego. Say, "Lord, I confess my hurt and my anger, and my hardness of heart toward You, because you did not do what I expected, but now forgive me."

Remember, forgiveness is ongoing because once you've dealt with the past, constant infractions occur in the present. None of us get by without having our pride wounded or being manipulated, offended, or hurt by someone. Each time that happens it leaves a scar on the soul if not confessed and dealt with before the Lord.

Pray the Scriptures

Father, I am struggling to forgive (name specific person or situation). I know it's Your will for me to forgive myself and others and I ask for Your help to do so. I pray I will forgive others as You have forgiven me (Ephesians 4:32). Help me to understand the lengths which Christ went to on the cross so my sins could be forgiven (Romans 5:8). Help me to model Jesus' example of forgiveness. I know forgiveness is a choice and one that I will have to make over and over again. Teach me to commit to a lifestyle of forgiveness.

Look over the scriptures you studied today and let them guide you as you write your own prayer below that addresses your specific needs.

A PRAYER TO
Obey God

How many times do we ask God to give us what we want, but we don't want to give God what He wants? We lack what we desire most—wholeness, peace, fulfillment, and joy—because we are not obedient to God. Often we are not obedient because we don't understand that God has set up certain rules to protect us and work for our benefit. The Ten Commandments were not given to instill guilt, but as an umbrella of blessing and protection from the rain of evil. If we choose to live outside the arena of blessing, spiritual darkness and confusion have access to our lives, and we are drained of God's best. When we obey, life has simplicity and clarity and unlimited blessing.

Key Scripture

"Do you not know that to whom you present yourselves slaves to obey, you are that one's slaves whom you obey, whether of sin leading to death, or of obedience leading to righteousness?" (Romans 6:16).

Prepare to Pray

We need God's laws because we don't know how to make life work without them. The Bible says, "If anyone competes in athletics, he is not crowned unless he competes according to the rules" (2 Timothy 2:5). If restoration is the name of the game, then obedience is one of the rules. The more I've searched the Scriptures, the more I've found that the Bible is full of promises for those who obey God:

- There is the promise of healing. "Make straight paths for your feet, so that what is lame may not be dislocated, but rather be healed" (Hebrews 12:13).
- There is the promise of answered prayer. "If I had cherished sin in my heart, the Lord would not have listened" (Psalm 66:18 NIV).
- There is the promise of living a long life in peace. "Let your heart keep my commands; for length of days and long life and peace they will add to you" (Proverbs 3:1–2).

Study the Scriptures

- Look up and read Deuteronomy 28:1–14. What correlation do you see between obeying God and blessing?

- Read Deuteronomy 28:15–19. What was the result when the Israelites disobeyed God?

- Obeying God doesn't mean we will get everything we want and that our lives will be free of hurt or suffering. But obeying God keeps us in the center of His good and perfect will. In your own words, how would you describe the benefits of obeying God?

- In what specific areas do you struggle with obeying God?

- Look up the following passages and consider how they relate to obeying God. How can you apply these truths to your own life?

Psalm 81:13–14	
Acts 5:29	

Romans 2:8	
2 Timothy 2:5	
1 Peter 1:22–23	

Respond to God's Word

I've learned that God doesn't enforce obedience. We often wish He would because it would be easier, but He gives us the choice. I had to ask Him to teach me to be obedient out of love for Him and desire to serve the One who has done so much for me. If you want the same benefits, you'll have to do the same thing. It helps to understand that the Lord is on your side and the call to obedience is not to make you feel like a hopeless failure if you don't do everything right.

The minute we take one step of obedience, God opens up opportunities for new life. Unfortunately, the opposite is also true. The minute we start to think it's not necessary to obey, we have opened the door for evil. For anyone who has been emotionally wounded in any way, a certain amount of healing will happen in your life just by being obedient to God. The Bible says, "Whoever keeps commandments keeps their life" (Proverbs 19:16 NIV). The more obedient you are, the more bondage will be stripped away from your life.

Pray the Scriptures

Father, I love You and I want to obey You. I know Your laws are for my good and contribute to my wholeness and well-being. I also know that disobedience only brings me grief and suffering. I pray that my heart will keep Your commands and I will enjoy a long, peaceful life (Proverbs 3:1–2). Help me to see areas where I am not obeying You and make me quick to confess and repent of my sins (1 John 1:9). I pray You will remove anything and everything in me that is offensive or unpleasing to You. Lord, I pray that the words of my mouth and meditations of my heart would be pleasing in Your sight (Psalm 19:14) and that I will be quick to obey Your good and righteous commands.

Look over the scriptures you studied today and let them guide you as you write your own prayer below that addresses your specific needs.

A PRAYER TO
Say Yes to God Each Day of Your Life

When you buy a house, you first make a large down payment. Then, to keep the house, you must make a smaller payment every time it comes due. You can't change your mind and say, "I don't feel like making payments!" without serious consequences. The same is true of your relationship with God. To make Him your permanent dwelling place, your initial down payment consists of making Him Lord over your life. After that, ongoing payments must be made, which means saying yes whenever God directs you to do something. They are all a part of the purchase, but one happens initially and the other is eternally ongoing (just like house payments!). The difference is that the Lord will take only as much payment from me as I am willing to give Him. And I can possess only as much of what He has for me as I am willing to secure with my obedience.

Taking the initial step of making Him Lord over your life is the same for everyone. Saying yes to God every day is an individual matter. God gives you personalized direction, so He may ask you to do something He is not asking anyone else to do. And "saying yes" to God is a decision you will make every day for the rest of your life.

Key Scripture

"If anyone desires to come after Me, let him deny himself, and take up his cross daily, and follow Me. For whoever desires to save his life will lose it, but whoever loses his life for My sake will save it" (Luke 9:23–24).

Prepare to Pray

Saying yes to God means being willing to obey immediately when we hear His voice, and not waiting until all else fails or we feel like it or we're at the end of ourselves. For God to transform us into whole people, we have to be totally available to Him. If He is telling us, "Do this," then our saying, "Yes, God" immediately will bring the desired results more quickly. Again, this is done a step at a time. If you can't trust God enough yet to say, "Anything You ask of me, I'll do," then keep working at it. I must admit that saying yes to God was difficult for me until I read God's words in the Scriptures: "When I called, they did not listen; so when they called, I would not listen" (Zechariah 7:13 NIV). That puts it all in perspective, doesn't it? There's nothing in this world that's worth hindering your relationship with God. The wise thing to do is make up your mind that you are going to "say yes" to God and obey Him no matter the circumstances.

Study the Scriptures

- Look up and read Matthew 7:24–27. What did Jesus say the outcome would be for those who obey His Word?

- In the same passage, how does Jesus describe the outcome for those who disobey His Word?

- Why do you think Jesus uses the example of building a house on rock or sand? How does rock and sand represent the difference between obedience and disobedience?

- Have you ever struggled to "say yes" to something God was asking of you? What was the outcome?

- Look up the following passages and consider how they relate to saying yes to God. How can you apply these truths to your own life?

1 Samuel 12:14–15	
Jeremiah 7:28	
Isaiah 50:10	
Hosea 4:9–10	

Respond to God's Word

If there's an area in your life where you're struggling to obey or "say yes" to something God is calling you to do, I encourage you to pray about it. Ask God to align your heart to His will. Confess your misgivings and tell God about your fears. It's important to remember that God doesn't ask us to obey to be restrictive or keep things from us—there is freedom found in obedience to His commands. Everything God forbids is for our safety and well-being. And everything He asks of us ultimately leads to His blessing and experiencing a greater measure of His presence and provision.

If we want God to hear our prayers, we need to listen and respond to His voice. Saying yes to God without reservation is the first step of obedience that begins to build a successful and fulfilling life on the foundation you have laid down in the Word: prayer, confession, praise, and ongoing forgiveness.

Pray the Scriptures

Father, give me the grace I need to take up my cross each day and follow You (Luke 9:23). I know if I insist on having my own way, my life will be diminished and lesser than it could be, but if I obey and follow You I will enjoy the abundant life You want me to have (Luke 9:24). Help me be quick to listen (Zechariah 7:13) and quick to say yes to whatever You ask of me. Help me to listen for Your voice and be quick to obey Your promptings. I want to obey Your Word and live in the center of Your will for my life.

Look over the scriptures you studied today and let them guide you as you write your own prayer below that addresses your specific needs.

A PRAYER TO
Resist the World and Ungodly Influences

Learning to live in the world without being influenced by evil is part of the process of becoming a mature Christ follower. Actually, it's so important it was one of the things Jesus prayed on behalf of His followers just before going to the cross. You can read Jesus' whole prayer—known as the High Priestly Prayer—in John 17. One of the things Jesus asked of the Father in this prayer was to protect His followers from evil. Jesus prayed, "I do not pray that You should take them out of the world, but that You should keep them from the evil one. They are not of the world, just as I am not of the world" (verses 15–16).

The world's influence can be subtle, but left unchecked it has the impact of a tsunami. Christians seldom say to themselves, *I am going to give in to the world's influence.* But still, without intentionality, it happens. One of the best ways to keep from being influenced by worldly evil is to commit to prayer and God's Word.

Key Scripture

"Do not be conformed to this world, but be transformed by the renewing of your mind, that you may prove what is that good and acceptable and perfect will of God" (Romans 12:2).

Prepare to Pray

Breaking from the world doesn't require you to live like a hermit for the rest of your life. But you do have to run a frequent check on your heart to make sure that you are not too attached to the world. One of the ways you can tell if you are submitting more to the ways of the world than the way of God is to ask yourself the following questions:

- Do I judge myself by the world's standard for beauty, acceptability, and success?
- Do I depend on worldly influencers and media to tell me how to live?
- Am I willing to ignore certain convictions I have in order to find favor with other people?
- Am I drawn toward emulating in any way the lifestyles of celebrities rather than becoming who God created me to be?
- Am I willing to compromise what I know of God's ways in order to gain something I want?

If you said yes to any of those questions, you are cutting off the possibilities God has for your life. God asks, "Since you died with Christ to the elemental spiritual forces of this world, why, as though you still belonged to the world, do you submit to its rules?" (Colossians 2:20 NIV).

Study the Scriptures

- Look up and read 1 John 2:15–17. How does the writer differentiate between the "things of the world" and the "things of the Father"?

- What comes to mind when you think of the term "worldly"?

- Glance back at 1 John 2:17. What is the future of "worldly things"?

- Romans 12:2 says, "Do not be conformed to this world, but be transformed by the renewing of your mind." What role do your thoughts play in confronting worldliness?

- Look up the following passages and consider how they relate to resisting ungodly influences. How can you apply these truths to your own life?

2 Timothy 2:22–26	
James 1:12–14	
1 Peter 1:15–16	
1 John 3:7–9	

Respond to God's Word

Our enemy is Satan, the ruler of this world, who was originally created beautiful, wise, and without sin. He had access to the throne of God, but fell from this high position when he chose to exert his will over God's. No one tempted him; he decided to rebel on his own. When his rebellion led to his expulsion from God's kingdom, he set himself to oppose all that God is and does. But Satan is limited. He cannot be everywhere, he is not able to do everything, he is not all-powerful, and he is not all-knowing.

God, on the other hand, is all of those things. What Satan and God do have in common is that they both have a plan for our lives, which can only be made operative if we submit to it. We don't have to fear Satan because the Bible says that "He who is in you is greater than he who is in the world" (1 John 4:4). Jesus' death on the cross has broken Satan's power, so we don't have to be intimidated by him.

Accepting the world's standards for our lives numbs our sensitivity to God's will. It separates us from what He has called us to be. We reserve a place in our hearts to be the exception. We think, *I'm above the Lord's ways. I don't need to obey*. But that is what Satan said before he fell from heaven.

The way we combat this deception is simple. The Bible says, "Submit to God. Resist the devil and he will flee from you" (James 4:7). We need to separate ourselves from the world's habits and ways of thinking and destroy the high places of our hearts. We must tell Satan we refuse to believe his lies or do things his way. When we refuse Satan, the promise is, "The Lord will go before you, and the God of Israel will be your rear guard" (Isaiah 52:12). The Lord will protect us from anything we may face ahead, and He will guard us against any dangers sneaking up from behind.

Pray the Scriptures

Father, I pray You will help me confront areas where I have been impacted by ungodly influences. Guard my mind from the worldly influences I see on social media, the news, and in my day-to-day dealings. I pray that I will not be conformed to this world, but that I will be transformed by the renewing of my mind (Romans 12:2). I pray that I will submit to You and that I will resist the devil (James 4:7).

Look over the scriptures you studied today and let them guide you as you write your own prayer below that addresses your specific needs.

A PRAYER FOR
Your Church Home

If you are already an active member at your church home, now is the time to start praying for your church and your pastor. If you don't yet have a church home, it is very important that you find a church home and spend time with that body of believers in church. I certainly understand if you have been hurt or burned out by a church, but please hear me out. No two churches are alike. Each has its own personality. Some are great, some good, and some not quite what you hoped they'd be. Somewhere there is a church that is right for you, and you need to ask God to help you find it. As you begin to pray to find the right church home, also ask God to bring godly friends into your life.

Key Scripture

"Oh come, let us worship and bow down; let us kneel before the LORD our Maker" (Psalm 95:6).

Prepare to Pray

Contrary to what some people think, the church doesn't have to have a fancy building. You can find a good church wherever a body of believers meets with a pastoral leader who is also submitted to other pastoral leadership. They must believe the Bible is the Word of God and offer good, solid teaching from it. The next important indication of a good church is that you sense the love of God there and you receive it in abundance from the people. If you go to a church that doesn't believe in being born again or being baptized, you need to find a church that does. Continue to look until you've found a solid church you can call home.

Go as often as you can. If once a week feels like a major commitment, start there. If once a week is easy, then go to midweek services also. Once you accept Jesus, you have eternal life whether you ever go to church or not, but I'm talking about living in the fullness of all God has for you. I'm talking about expelling the pain from deep within and living in love, peace, and joy. I'm talking about doing God's will. Certain visitations of God's power happen only in the midst of such gatherings of believers. Make it a point to be a part of that.

Study the Scriptures

- Look up and read Acts 2:42. What insight does this passage give to the priorities of the early church?

- How are the practices described in Acts 2:42 still beneficial to modern-day believers?

- How would you describe your level of participation and commitment to the local church? If you're not as active as you'd like to be, what steps can you take to get involved?

- Look up and read 1 Peter 5:8–9. This passage warns Christians to be aware of Satan's schemes and to resist him. Why is it helpful to know other believers are going through similar trials? Based on what you read in this passage, why is biblical community an important part of resisting Satan?

- Look up the following passages and consider how they reveal the importance of finding a church home. How can you apply these truths to your own life?

Proverbs 27:17	
Romans 12:9–13	
2 Corinthians 6:14–15	
Hebrews 10:24–25	
1 John 1:6–7	

Respond to God's Word

When you make friends with people who follow the Lord, there is a strong bond of love that makes other relationships seem shallow. Such friendships are the most fulfilling and healing. They can also be the most frustrating because we expect Christians to be perfect, when in reality only Christ is perfect. It's helpful to think of all fellowship with believers as beneficial: The pleasant encounters are healing and the unpleasant ones are stretching. When you run across believers who stretch you more than you feel you can handle, don't turn away from God. Remember, He is still perfect and good even if some of His children aren't. God always loves and respects you, even if a few of His offspring don't. I know that nothing hurts worse than a wound inflicted by a brother or sister in the Lord. Having been wounded many times like that myself, I am forced to remember that we will be imperfect until we go to be with Jesus. So we need to be merciful to those who "stretch" us and forgive quickly. Besides, we are probably stretching others ourselves.

Start somewhere. Make a phone call to another believer and ask for prayer. Meet someone for lunch and talk about what the Lord has done in your life. Open up and extend yourself in some way. You may feel you don't have anything to share, but if you have the Lord, He's all you need.

If our first goal in any relationship is our own fulfillment, we will ultimately be let down or disappointed. As painful as it is, we have to give up that desire and lay it at Jesus' feet. However, there may be times when we have done all we can do in a relationship and it is still filled with problems. As hard as we try to make things good, a certain person may always leave you feeling depressed, angry, insecure, frightened, or hurt. When that happens, it is best to let the friendship go and give it to God to restore or remove as He sees fit. Fellowship is a step of obedience that expands our hearts, bridges gaps, and breaks down walls. It encourages, fulfills, and balances our lives. All of this is necessary for spiritual well-being and a fruitful life in the will of God.

Pray the Scriptures

Father, I know it is Your will for me to be an active participant in biblical community (Hebrews 10:24–25). I pray You will lead me to a good church home where I can worship, serve, and experience good relationships. I pray for godly friends of Your choosing who will help me grow in my faith (Proverbs 27:17). I ask You to help me be a good friend to others and find others who will be good friends to me. Lord, help me remember that only Jesus is perfect. When my friends disappoint me, I pray You will help me be mindful that only Jesus can meet my needs and to extend grace in the way You have shown grace to me.

Look over the scriptures you studied today and let them guide you as you write your own prayer below that addresses your specific needs.

A PRAYER TO
Have a Biblical Attitude About Money

When I was ten years old, I lay awake in the middle of a cold, pitch-black night because I was too hungry to sleep. The pangs in my stomach were magnified by the knowledge that there was no food in the house and no money to buy any. Going hungry was terribly frightening. Having to be totally dependent for life and sustenance upon someone I couldn't depend on at all bred deep insecurity. Once I was out of school and self-supporting, I handled money very carefully. I felt the weight of being entirely responsible for my life, and the horror of someday starving to death always bubbled just below the surface of my mind.

After I came to know the Lord and started going to church, I put money in the collection plate according to what I had with me—a couple of dollars at first, then a five, a ten, and later a twenty. It was more like I was donating to a good cause or tipping the piano player than having any thought of actually giving to God. As I matured, I learned that giving was actually giving back to God out of what He had given me, and by doing so I would never lose anything. In fact, I would be enriched.

Key Scripture

"Bring all the tithes into the storehouse,
That there may be food in My house,
And try Me now in this,'
Says the Lord of hosts,

'If I will not open for you the windows of heaven
And pour out for you such blessing
That there will not be room enough to receive it'" (Malachi 3:10).

Prepare to Pray

The Bible teaches we are to give a tithe (10 percent) of our income to God. Because we can't separate our money from our lives, God must be made Lord over our finances, and we must obey Him. God says in His Word that we need to give a tenth of our earnings back to Him for His purposes. When we realize that every cent we have comes from God in the first place, that's not such an unreasonable request. A good steward of money realizes he has nothing on his own, but only manages what he has been given.

Study the Scriptures

- Look up and read Luke 6:38. What did Jesus mean when he said, "For with the same measure that you use, it will be measured back to you"?

- How would you describe your attitude about giving? Do you enjoy giving or do you find it difficult?

- Look up and read 2 Corinthians 9:7. What does this passage tell you about how God wants you to give?

- Have you ever been on the receiving end of a gift that was given begrudgingly? How does that experience differ from receiving from a cheerful giver?

- Look up the following passages and consider how they relate to having a biblical attitude about money. How can you apply these truths to your own life?

Deuteronomy 8:18	
Deuteronomy 15:10	
Malachi 3:10–12	
Psalm 41:1–3	
Proverbs 11:24–25	

Respond to God's Word

If we tithe, the Bible promises we will receive a multiplied return of God's abundance and His power. The Lord asks us to try Him and see if He is not faithful to provide more blessings than we can contain. When we cut ourselves off from this life principle, the devourer comes in to eat up everything we have. I see people who don't give and then lose what they could have given in medical bills, appliance and car repairs, and a general lack of power to change their lives. God still loves them, but they've stopped up the flow of His blessing to them. The only way the storehouse of God's abundance can be opened is for them to start the process by opening themselves up to giving.

We often feel we will lose something if we give. We think, *If I didn't have to give this, I would have more for myself.* But actually that attitude will cause us to lose. The Bible says that if we give to the Lord, we will have everything we need in our lives. If we don't, we won't. When we live in fear that we won't have enough, it's hard to give. But the truth is, the more we give to others, the more will be released to us. We will reap a spiritual as well as a material harvest. While it's good to save and plan wisely for the future because extreme poverty is emotionally crippling, giving to the Lord and to others must not be excluded. If we don't give as the Lord directs, we end up losing what we think we're saving anyway.

Pray the Scriptures

Lord, help me give the way You want me to, because I want to be obedient in this area of my life. Help me always tithe so that I am never robbing You of what is Yours (Malachi 3:9–10). I pray I will give with a cheerful and willing attitude (2 Corinthians 9:7). Lord, I am mindful of all You have given me in Christ Jesus. Every good gift I have has come from Your hand (Psalm 16:2). I want to live in the center of Your will so I can receive all You have for me and become all You made me to be. Lord, show me any area of need where I could give something of myself or what I have. Show me what I might release of my life into the life of another person, and help me to do it.

Look over the scriptures you studied today and let them guide you as you write your own prayer below that addresses your specific needs.

A PRAYER TO
Walk in Faith

If you want to have more faith, you are in good company. The Gospel of Luke tells us that Jesus' apostles longed for more faith too. So, what did they do? They asked Jesus for more faith! (17:5). If you want more faith, it's wise to make faith an ongoing prayer request. Faith is a spiritual muscle that needs to be exercised in order to prevent atrophy, which makes our entire spiritual being weak. Faith is first a decision, then an exercise in obedience, then a gift from God as it is multiplied. Our first step of faith is taken when we decide we will receive Jesus. After that, every time we decide to trust the Lord for anything, we build that faith. And whenever we decide not to trust Him, we tear it down.

Key Scripture

"And the apostles said to the Lord, 'Increase our faith'" (Luke 17:5).

Prepare to Pray

Faith is our daily decision to trust God. In the simplest terms, faith is believing God will do as He has said. The Bible says, "Whatever is not from faith is sin" (Romans 14:23). How much clearer can it be? Faith is obedience. Doubt is disobedience. Faith is a gift from God because

He enables us to believe, but we have to obey by building on that faith. Scripture also says that a person who doubts is unstable in every way and cannot please God. If that's true, spiritual well-being is not possible without faith, so it's important that you pray about your faith.

Study the Scriptures

- Look up and read Hebrews 11:6. According to this passage, why is faith so important?

- Glance back at the latter part of Hebrews 11:6. What will happen if you diligently seek God?

- This passage makes it clear that God rewards those who diligently seek Him. How does this passage encourage you? Practically speaking, what would it look like for you to diligently seek God?

- How would you describe your faith in this season of life? Are there any areas in which you are struggling? If so, write them down and include them in the prayer at the end of the study.

- Look up the following passages and consider how they relate to walking in faith. How can you apply these truths to your own life?

Proverbs 3:5	
Hebrews 4:2	
Hebrews 11:6	
James 1:2–3	
James 1:6–8	

Respond to God's Word

How do we start building faith? Once we have a little, how do we get more? The first step is to be totally open and honest about any doubt in God's ability or His faithfulness to provide for our every need. Pour your thoughts out to Him in prayer. If you are having trouble having faith in a specific area, confess that to God in prayer and ask God to help you. Remember, God wants you to be strong in faith and He delights to grow His children's faith when they ask Him. The next step is to fill your mind with the Word: "Faith comes from hearing the message, and the message is heard through the word about Christ" (Romans 10:17 NIV). Reading the Word daily, regularly submitting to Bible teaching, and speaking the Word aloud will build faith. Your mouth and heart have to be united in this. One can't be saying, "God can," while the other says, "God can't." Your mind will convince your heart as you read or speak God's Word.

Whenever I'm afraid or doubt that my life is secure, I read the Bible until I sense God's peace in me. The more I read, the more hope I have. Then, when I pray, I'm confident that God will answer my prayers. Even if you are not given to fear and doubt, you can be attacked by a spirit of doubt, as I was. When that happens, don't carry it by yourself. Take it to the Lord immediately. Or ask a mature believer to pray with you if you need to. Sensing your own limitations doesn't mean you don't have faith. Feeling that God has limitations is what indicates a lack of faith. When faith has blossomed, it gives birth to hope, and says, "There is an end to this. I won't be in this situation forever. I won't always feel like this. I won't always hurt." Hope and faith together give you a vision for your life. The Bible says of the people who could not go into the promised land, "They could not enter in because of unbelief" (Hebrews 3:19). Don't let that happen to you. Choose to enter in to all that God has for you by taking this important step of obedience.

Pray the Scriptures

God, Your Word says that without faith it is impossible to please You, but that You will reward those who diligently seek You (Hebrews 11:6). Lord, I am seeking You now and will continue with diligence. Just like Jesus' apostles, I ask, "Lord, increase my faith" (Luke 17:5). Jesus, I confess that when I'm afraid, I'm prone to unbelief. I ask that You protect me from doubt (James 1:2–3). I pray that when I hear Your Word preached and read the Scriptures that my faith will grow and mature (Romans 10:17).

Look over the scriptures you studied today and let them guide you as you write your own prayer below that addresses your specific needs.

A PRAYER FOR
Your Mind

I was always afraid that I would inherit my mother's predisposition to mental illness, so when I started having some frightening thoughts after I was in counseling, I told my counselor, "Sometimes I feel like I'm losing my mind."

My counselor said I was being mentally oppressed, which is quite different from being mentally ill. "You've been delivered from major oppression, but you still must choose to let the mind of Christ control you. You've started allowing yourself to listen to whatever thoughts come into your mind."

I grew up with a mother whose every wild thought controlled her, so it had never occurred to me that I could choose my thoughts. But the Bible makes it clear we are not to conform to the world's way of thinking (Romans 12:2). It says we are to renew our minds by taking captive every thought to make it obedient to Christ (2 Corinthians 10:5). God has also made clear what we are to allow into our minds. "Whatever is true, whatever is noble, whatever is right, whatever is pure, whatever is lovely, whatever is admirable—if anything is excellent or praiseworthy—think about such things" (Philippians 4:8 NIV).

Key Scripture

"'Who has known the mind of the LORD that he may instruct Him?' But we have the mind of Christ" (1 Corinthians 2:16).

Prepare to Pray

I've found that the best way to control my thoughts is to control my outside influences. For instance, how many times have you seen something on TV or social media that negatively influenced your thoughts? That's because whatever goes into your mind affects your emotions. You have to be specific about what you allow into your mind and truly take every thought captive. King David knew how much our minds control our thoughts. And he knew that God was aware of our thoughts. In Psalm 139 he prayed:

> O Lord, You have searched me and known me . . .
> You understand my thought afar off.
> You comprehend my path and my lying down,
> And are acquainted with all my ways . . .
> You have hedged me behind and before,
> And laid Your hand upon me. (verses 1–3, 5)

Study the Scriptures

- Read Philippians 4:8. Notice how the apostle Paul instructs readers to think on what is "true." In your experience, what are some of the typical pitfalls in which you think about things that are "untrue"? Ask God to show you if you aren't sure.

- **What does Paul mean when he instructs readers to "meditate on these things"?**

- **In varying degree, everyone struggles with their thoughts. In what areas do you tend to struggle (worry, rehearsing past mistakes, imagining worst-case scenarios, replaying past harms and offenses)? Write down areas you need to pray about.**

- **Generally, what impact are your thoughts having on your life?**

- **Look up the following passages and consider how they relate to your mind. How can you apply these truths to your own life?**

1 Chronicles 28:9	
Romans 12:2	
2 Corinthians 10:3–5	
Philippians 4:8	

Respond to God's Word

It's good to evaluate your state of mind frequently to see if your thoughts are in line with the Lord's. Stop now and take an inventory of your thoughts by reviewing the statements below that apply to you:

- "My thoughts make me feel sad, depressed, lonely, or hopeless."
- "My thoughts cause me to be angry, bitter, or unforgiving."
- "My thoughts cause me to feel self-hatred and self-doubt."
- "My thoughts bring feelings of anxiety or fear."
- "I often think of negative memories."
- "I sometimes think of immoral sexual images."
- "I rarely think of positive things."

If you answered yes to any of these questions, you are living with needless torment, and it's time to take charge of your mind. Scripture says, "For the word of God is alive and active . . . it judges the thoughts and attitudes of the heart. Nothing in all creation is hidden from God's sight. Everything is uncovered and laid bare before the eyes of him to whom we must give account" (Hebrews 4:12–13 NIV).

The main weapon in mental warfare is to deliberately feed your mind with God's truth and power. Fill your mind with His Word as you work through the different steps in our journey together. Seek out Christian books and magazines. Play Christian music in your home and your car. Put on worship music and turn it loud enough to drown out the negative voices in your mind. Some movies, music, books, and television programs may not be saying "Jesus is Lord," but they are based on Christian principles and have a Christian spirit behind them. Seek out those things. And if you are watching or listening to something that is negative or immoral, turn it off.

Pray the Scriptures

God, I know You are aware of what goes on in my thought life (Psalm 139:1–3). I pray that I will be intentional about my thoughts and think about what is true, noble, just, pure, lovely, and praiseworthy (Philippians 4:8). Help me to take every thought captive and make my thoughts obedient to Christ (2 Corinthians 10:5). I pray I will not be conformed to the ways of this world but that I will transformed by the renewing of my mind (Romans 12:2). Help me to avoid "what-ifs" and worst-case-scenario type thinking. Instead, help my thoughts be filled with faith and hope. Call to mind the ways You have been faithful.

Look over the scriptures you studied today and let them guide you as you write your own prayer below that addresses your specific needs.

A PRAYER FOR

Sexual Healing and Purity

With the prevalence of sexual promiscuity and internet pornography there are millions of people who are in desperate need of sexual healing. If you find yourself in this situation, you are far from alone. But sexual sin isn't something to take lightly. Just because it's common doesn't mean it's not sin and displeasing to God. Some people fall into the trap of believing that sex outside of marriage is OK as long as they are in a committed relationship, but that is not true. Sexual immorality is having sex with anyone to whom you are not married. God's plan for sex is intended for a man and woman in the context of marriage. Genesis 2:24 says, "Therefore a man shall leave his father and mother and be joined to his wife, and they shall become one flesh."

People are usually sexually immoral because they either believe there is nothing wrong with it, or they are so in need of closeness, love, and affirmation, they don't have the power to say no. But sex outside of marriage will never be the committed, sacrificial, unconditional love we really need. Sexual immorality is not just a physical encounter; it invades the soul. Sexual joining unites one person with another. When the relationship is broken, a part of the personality of each person is chipped away. Many such involvements cause many chips. By the time the person finds the one she's supposed to be with, she is so fragmented that she doesn't have a whole person to offer. Sexual immorality scars our souls and damages our emotions more severely than any other disobedience.

Key Scripture

"Have mercy upon me, O God,
According to Your lovingkindness;
According to the multitude of Your tender mercies,
Blot out my transgressions.
Wash me thoroughly from my iniquity,
And cleanse me from my sin"
(Psalm 51:1–2).

Prepare to Pray

The road back from such sexual sin can be slow because the fragmentation of the soul is deeper than any caused by other sins. The Bible says, "He who commits sexual immorality sins against his own body" (1 Corinthians 6:18). I know how difficult this step of obedience is, especially for someone who is emotionally needy or who has suffered hurt, rejection, or a lack of love. Fortunately, we have a God who understands how difficult it is. All He asks is that we have a heart that says, "I want to do what's right. God, help me to do it."

Study the Scriptures

- Look up and read 1 Corinthians 6:18. Why do you think the apostle Paul uses the word "flee" when he describes how to deal with sexual immorality?

- According to this passage, how does sexual sin differ from other types of sins?

- Why do you think the impact of sexual sin tends to linger unless you've confessed and repented?

- Is there anything you need to confess? Any areas where you need God's healing from past sins?

- Look up the following passages and consider how they relate to sexual purity. How can you apply these truths to your own life?

Psalm 51:6–7	
Matthew 5:32	
1 Corinthians 5:1	
1 Corinthians 6:13	

Respond to God's Word

How about you? Have you sinned in this area? Ask God to forgive you for this sin. Then ask Him to help you remain pure in the future. Remember to be mindful that you will deal with the possibility that you may be tempted by lust in the future. Once you have confessed your past sexual sins to God; those sins are forgiven. But you need to pray and ask God to help you to continue to walk in His ways. Remember, the Bible says:

"No temptation has overtaken you except such as is common to man; but God is faithful, who will not allow you to be tempted beyond what you are able, but with the temptation will also make the way of escape, that you may be able to bear it" (1 Corinthians 10:13).

Sometimes sexual sin isn't your fault. If you were raped, assaulted, trafficked, or abused, you have been impacted by someone else's sin. God hates sexual violence and coercion. If you feel tainted by sexual impurity because of acts that were not your choice, God wants you to be released from the burden of them. I encourage you to pray to be released from feelings of shame and impurity. Don't hesitate to reach out to a godly therapist and seek counseling. It's God's will for you to be healed from the negative feelings you are experiencing.

Pray the Scriptures

Father, Your Word says if I confess my sins, You will be faithful to forgive me and purify me from all unrighteousness (1 John 1:9). I confess that I have sinned (name specific situations). I ask for Your forgiveness in Jesus' name and ask You to purify me. Lord, if and when I am tempted in the future I pray I will respond in a godly way. I want to live my life in a way that is pleasing to You. I pray You will free me from the guilt and shame that come from sexual sin. Help me to walk in sexual purity from now on.

Look over the scriptures you studied today and let them guide you as you write your own prayer below that addresses your specific needs.

A PRAYER FOR

When You're Fasting

God designed fasting to bring us into a deeper knowledge of Him, to release the Holy Spirit's work in our lives, and to bring us to greater spiritual wholeness. In fact, the Bible says certain spirits can only be broken through fasting. When Jesus' disciples asked why evil spirits didn't submit to them, He replied, "This kind can come out by nothing but prayer and fasting" (Mark 9:29).

Key Scripture

"Then Jesus was led up by the Spirit into the wilderness to be tempted by the devil. And when He had fasted forty days and forty nights, afterward He was hungry" (Matthew 4:1–2).

Prepare to Pray

Fasting is designed "to loose the bonds of wickedness, to undo the heavy burdens" (Isaiah 58:6). Who doesn't need the power of God to penetrate her life and circumstances? So what's holding us back? I believe it's ignorance and fear. We are ignorant of what the Bible says on the subject, and of what fasting can accomplish, and of all of its wonderful benefits. And we are afraid of the discomfort that can accompany infrequent fasts. Yet there are more than eighty references to fasting in the Old and New Testaments. Jesus Himself fasted for forty days and forty nights in the wilderness. Fasting is a spiritual exercise and discipline during which you give yourself completely to prayer and close communion with God. It's a time to sensitize your soul to His Spirit and to see Him work mightily on your behalf.

Study the Scriptures

- Look up and read Matthew 6:16–18. Notice that Jesus said, "When you fast . . ." Why is it significant that Jesus said "when" rather than "if"? What does this imply?

- What instructions did Jesus give about fasting?

- What benefits can you see in fasting?

- If you haven't fasted before, what's holding you back?

- **Look up the following passages and consider how they relate to fasting and prayer. How can you apply these truths to your own life?**

Isaiah 58:1–14	
Psalm 35:11–13	
Psalm 69:5–19	
Colossians 4:2	

Respond to God's Word

Once you are convinced of the rightness of fasting, you need to take the first step. Begin by simply skipping a meal, drinking water, and praying at the time you would ordinarily eat. Say, "God, I fast this meal to Your glory and to the breaking down of strongholds in my life." Then lift up in prayer all the areas where you know you need freedom. Say, for example, "Lord, I fast this day for breaking down strongholds the devil has erected in my mind through depression, confusion, unforgiveness, or anger."

The next time, try skipping two meals. Then see if you can work up to a full twenty-four- to thirty-six-hour water fast once a week. I fast about forty days a year, but I do it one day a week for forty weeks. I actually look forward to it as a time to hear God more clearly. If you have a physical limitation and cannot water fast, then go on a vegetable or fruit fast, denying yourself everything but vegetables or fruits for a day.

In Isaiah 58 God gives guidelines for fasting by examining the Israelites' current practices. The people were fasting, all right, but they were not "walking the walk"; their actions did not show any follow-through. God says if your fasting is going to please Him you should:

- Stop oppressing those who work for you. Treat them fairly (verse 6).
- Share your food with the hungry and welcome wanderers into your home (verse 7).
- Keep the Sabbath day holy (verse 13).

In other words, walk your talk! I recommend that you read the entire chapter of Isaiah 58 each time you fast to remind yourself of exactly why you are fasting (to be free), what you are to do (give of yourself), and what your rewards are (healing, answered prayer, deliverance, and protection). Almost everywhere fasting is mentioned in Scripture, prayer accompanies the discipline. Fasting can only be effective if it humbles us before God and brings closer communication with Him.

Be sure to accompany your fast with prayer. Fasting without prayer is just starvation. This is a time to be close to the Lord and to allow Him to guide you where you need to go. Sometimes you will have the clear leading of the Holy Spirit as to why you are fasting; sometimes you won't.

Whether you do or not, it's good to have a prayer focus in mind. Remember that "no discipline seems pleasant at the time, but painful. Later on, however, it produces a harvest of righteousness and peace for those who have been trained by it" (Hebrews 12:11 NIV).

Pray the Scriptures

Father, I recognize that Jesus is the model set for all Christians. The Bible teaches that Jesus fasted (Matthew 4). I pray I will make fasting a part of my spiritual practices and by fasting I will draw near to You. Help me to approach fasting with pure motives. I don't want to fast to draw attention to myself but rather to devote to obeying Your Word and advancing Your kingdom (Matthew 6:16–18). Jesus said some problems can only be addressed by prayer and fasting (Mark 9:29). Give me wisdom and guidance to know how to fast, Lord. Enable me to do it.

Look over the scriptures you studied today and let them guide you as you write your own prayer below that addresses your specific needs.

A PRAYER FOR
When You're Struggling with Confusion

Lots of confusion exists in the world today because what is bad is now considered good, and what is good is disdained. Life has become bewildering, and the only thing that breaks through the confusion is the Lord's presence and the Word of His truth. Too many outside opinions, when you should be listening only to God's, will cause confusion. Opposing God's Word in any way will cause confusion to dwell in your life.

When sex, money, and power become idols in our lives, we will live in chaos and confusion. In fact, all lust of the flesh brings confusion: "Where envy and self-seeking exist, confusion and every evil thing are there" (James 3:16). When God is completely in charge of every area of your life, clarity, simplicity, and peace are the immediate by-products. If not, life becomes jumbled, out of order, complex, and confusing. If you are feeling confused today, take an inventory of your situation to determine where it's coming from.

Key Scripture

"God is not the author of confusion but of peace" (1 Corinthians 14:33).

Prepare to Pray

God does sometimes use confusion to punish those who are disobedient and to destroy His enemies. He warned the Israelites about this. Before the Jewish people entered the promised land, Moses stopped them at the Jordan River to review the law with this new generation. He and the Levitical priests spoke both the blessings the Israelites would receive in the promised land if they obeyed—and the curses that would be upon them if they disobeyed.

Moses said, "The LORD will send on you cursing, confusion, and rebuke in all that you set your hand to do, until you are destroyed and until you perish quickly, because of the wickedness of your doings in which you have forsaken Me . . . The LORD will strike you with madness and blindness and confusion of heart" (Deuteronomy 28:20, 28). The good news is, that God also provides wisdom, peace, clarity, and guidance for those who choose to seek His guidance and walk in His ways.

Study the Scriptures

- Look up and read Psalm 119:105. According to the psalmist, what brings light, clarity, and direction?

- Write down the areas where you are dealing with confusion. Does the Bible speak directly about these issues?

- If you're dealing with confusion, one thing to remember is that God will never lead you to do anything that is in violation of His Word. But it's necessary to listen and be attentive to ways He is leading. Look up and read Psalm 32:8. What does this passage say God will do for those who seek Him?

- Look up and read James 1:5. What does this passage say about God's willingness to give wisdom to those who ask?

- Look up the following passages and consider how they relate to confronting confusion. How can you apply these truths to your own life?

Isaiah 40:28–31	
Jeremiah 20:11	
Psalm 35:4	
Psalm 35:26	
James 3:14–16	

Respond to God's Word

When you are dealing with confusion, it may cause you to make unwise or quick decisions based on incorrect information. But remember, you absolutely never have to live with confusion. Take it to God in prayer. Ask God to reveal if you have been disobedient in any way that has allowed a spirit of confusion to come into your life. If that's the case, confess and repent of your disobedience. If that's not the case, ask God to show you if any confusion in your life is from the Enemy. If that's the case, rebuke the spirit of confusion, saying, "By the authority I have in Jesus Christ I command the spirit of confusion to be gone."

Then begin to worship and praise God until you are thinking clearly again. Confusion cannot coexist with God's presence and obedience to His laws. That's why worship, praise, and thanksgiving are the best weapons to dissolve it. Remember that prayer is one of the primary ways to deal with spiritual warfare. The apostle Paul wrote:

> Finally, my brethren, be strong in the Lord and in the power of His might. Put on the whole armor of God, that you may be able to stand against the wiles of the devil. For we do not wrestle against flesh and blood, but against principalities, against powers, against the rulers of the darkness of this age, against spiritual hosts of wickedness in the heavenly places. Therefore take up the whole armor of God, that you may be able to withstand in the evil day, and having done all, to stand. Stand therefore, having girded your waist with truth, having put on the breastplate of righteousness, and having shod your feet with the preparation of the gospel of peace; above all, taking the shield of faith with which you will be able to quench all the fiery darts of the wicked one. And take the helmet of salvation, and the sword of the Spirit, which is the word of God; praying always with all prayer and supplication in the Spirit, being watchful to this end with all perseverance and supplication for all the saints. (Ephesians 6:10–18)

Pray the Scriptures

Father, Your Word says You are not the author of confusion but of peace (1 Corinthians 14:33). I don't want anything in my life that is not authored by You. Father, show me any behavior that I may have engaged in that might have brought confusion into my life. I confess (name any known sins) and ask for Your forgiveness in Jesus' name (1 John 1:9). Lord, I ask You for wisdom (James 1:5) and pray You will guide me. Father, if I get off Your path for me, I pray You will quickly redirect my steps.

Look over the scriptures you studied today and let them guide you as you write your own prayer below that addresses your specific needs.

A PRAYER TO

Heal from a Critical Spirit

Those of us who have been neglected, abused, or mistreated as children often grow up to be judgmental and critical. Being torn down when we were young makes tearing someone else down to build ourselves up very appealing. Yet constantly criticizing someone else, even in our minds, invites a critical spirit. Our every thought and word is colored by it and having a critical spirit brings consequences. We eventually become cynical and completely unable to experience joy. Criticism crowds out love in our hearts. And without love, we cannot grow emotionally.

Key Scripture

"Let no corrupt word proceed out of your mouth, but what is good for necessary edification, that it may impart grace to the hearers" (Ephesians 4:29).

Prepare to Pray

I used to be very critical of people, mentally dissecting them to see if they were better than I was, as I feared. Then I read in my Bible, "For with what judgment you judge, you will be judged; and with the measure you use, it will be measured back to you" (Matthew 7:2). Judging people was inviting judgment upon myself. This is the lie we want to believe when we criticize others: "I'm better than they are." But what we really fear is this: "They are better than I am." The deception we come under is thinking that anyone but God has the right to sit in judgment of another person.

Not only do we not have a right to judge, but if we are mindful of all the ways God has forgiven us of our sins, we will become increasingly gracious and merciful. The apostle Paul wrote, "Who are you to judge another's servant? To his own master he stands or falls. Indeed, he will be made to stand, for God is able to make him stand" (Romans 14:4). Avoiding a critical spirit doesn't mean that we don't recognize or speak up when something is immoral or wrong. But it does mean that we look at things through the lens of people who have been forgiven and are following in the path of our Savior, Jesus Christ. The Bible describes Jesus as being filled with grace and truth (John 1:14). So when we do have to confront hard things, we do it with grace, love, and kindness.

Study the Scriptures

- Look up and read Numbers 12. Why did Miriam speak critically about her brother Moses?

- How did God respond to Miriam's critical spirit (verses 9–10)?

- **Have you ever experienced consequences for speaking poorly about someone?**

- **What did Moses pray on Miriam's behalf? How did God answer?**

- **Look up the following passages and consider how they relate to a critical spirit. How can you apply these truths to your own life?**

Zechariah 8:17	
John 8:7	
Ephesians 4:29–32	
James 3:16–17	
1 Peter 4:8	

Respond to God's Word

Moses' sister, Miriam, who was a leader of the Hebrews, unfortunately fell into the pitfall of criticism. She and her brother Aaron criticized Moses for choosing an Ethiopian wife they didn't think was suitable for him. God confronted Miriam and Aaron for their critical spirit. He began by showing them how wrong they were to criticize this godly man. He told them Moses was a faithful man. "I speak to him face to face, clearly, and not in riddles! He sees the LORD as he is. So why were you not afraid to criticize my servant Moses?" (Numbers 12:8 NLT).

God didn't give Miriam time to answer His question. He quickly departed, and Miriam was left a leprous outcast. Moses interceded for his sister (after all, she helped save him from Pharaoh's decree of death to all Hebrew baby boys). And Miriam's punishment was limited to seven days outside the camp as a leper, rather than a life of this dreaded disease.

Moses prayed for Miriam and God healed her. But having a critical spirit carries built-in consequences like stealing our joy, thwarting our love, and giving us a reputation as someone who speaks poorly of others. We all need to avoid having a critical spirit. Typical behavioral characteristics that accompany a critical spirit include complaining, inability to show gratitude, identifying everything that is wrong and never taking the time to celebrate what is right, talking negatively about other people, speaking up about things that are none of our business, and being vocal about how you would do things differently than another person. If you have a critical spirit, I encourage you to make it a priority in prayer. It's not God's will for you to continue with a critical spirit and He will help you if you seek Him.

Pray the Scriptures

Father, Your Word warns against having a judgmental and critical spirit, and I ask You to deliver me from any areas where I am prone to that behavior. I confess (list any known sins). I have fallen short in this area and I ask for Your forgiveness. Help me speak words that encourage others. I pray my words will be filled with grace (Ephesians 4:29). When I have to confront hard situations, I pray my words will be like Jesus' and filled with grace and truth (John 1:14). Give me wisdom to know when to speak up and when it's better to stay quiet. But when I speak, I pray my words will be kind and helpful.

Look over the scriptures you studied today and let them guide you as you write your own prayer below that addresses your specific needs.

A PRAYER FOR
When You're Depressed

Many years ago, I used to wake up every morning with a familiar, gnawing ache. I would think, *This is just the way I am.* Yet since I have come to know the Lord, I have never felt this hopelessness again. As I look back, I see that I didn't have to live like that, and I wonder how many people still live with this kind of distress. It's so familiar, and they are so used to living with these feelings that they think it's part of their lives.

Believing we cannot live with our situation the way it is—and that we are powerless to change it—causes discouragement to settle over us like a thick fog, and we can't see any way out of the darkness. The deception is thinking that our situation is hopeless.

Key Scripture

"Why are you cast down, O my soul?
And why are you disquieted within me?
Hope in God, for I shall yet praise Him
For the help of His countenance"
(Psalm 42:5).

Prepare to Pray

If you struggle with depression, you are not alone. Depression doesn't discriminate and it impacts all kinds of people. Some of the people God used in mighty ways in Scripture suffered from depression; Elijah, King David, Jeremiah, and Asaph all dealt with depression. If you suffer from depression, it might be necessary to seek out a godly therapist who can point you in the right direction. God has gifted people with a wide variety of skills and knowledge regarding mental health and there are people who can help you recover.

Your spiritual life will also play a big role in treating depression. God understands your thoughts, feelings, and emotions better than anyone and He has compassion for your suffering. If you take a close look at Scripture, you'll see that many of God's servants were forthcoming with God about how low they felt and they didn't hold anything back from Him. As you learn to pray the Scriptures, you'll see that there's nothing you can't take to God in prayer.

Study the Scriptures

- Look up and read Psalm 77. This psalm was written by a man named Asaph. In verses 1–10, what evidence do you see that Asaph is depressed?

- Glance back at verse 4. Why do you think Asaph is having trouble sleeping and is struggling to verbalizing his feelings?

- In verses 11–12, there's a shift in Asaph's thoughts. What does Asaph begin to think about in verses 11–12? Can you recall some of the ways God has worked in your life? Write down answered prayers, and other ways you've seen God work.

- Look over verses 13–20. How does Asaph's mood change? What is the result of his mood change?

- Look up the following passages and consider how they relate to depression. How can you apply these truths to your own life?

Jeremiah 31:3–4	
Psalm 34:4–5	
Ephesians 2:8–10	

Philippians 1:6	
Philippians 4:6–7	

Respond to God's Word

In the opening lines of Psalm 77, it's obvious that Asaph was feeling low. In Asaph's despair, he "cried out to God" (verse 1). The text makes it clear that he didn't hold anything back and even asked, "Has God forgotten to be gracious? Has He in anger shut up His tender mercies?" (verse 9). When you're depressed, it's not uncommon to wonder if God is angry or if He has forgotten you. But Asaph took those worries to God in prayer. And when Asaph shifted his thoughts to all the ways God had worked in the past, his mood began to change. When his thoughts began to change, his mood changed, and then his words changed. If you look closely, you'll see that Asaph's words shifted from lament (verses 1–10) to praise and worship (verses 11–20).

Our thoughts have a profound impact on our moods. One of the primary ways you can influence your thoughts is by taking in a steady diet of God's Word. That might come in the form of listening to godly preaching, reading your Bible, attending a small group Bible study, memorizing Scripture, listening to praise and worship music, and reading godly books. Also, it's a good idea to think about your history with God. Spend some time recalling the ways He's helped you in the past. He's gotten you this far, hasn't He? Rehearsing your history with God will stir your faith and bring to mind all the ways He's been faithful to bring you through hard seasons in the past. Thinking about those things will stir your faith that He will continue to be faithful in the future.

Pray the Scriptures

Father, I thank You because Your Word describes You as a God who redeems my life from destruction, and crowns me with lovingkindness and tender mercies (Psalm 103:4). I praise You, Lord, because You are merciful and gracious (Psalm 103:8). Jesus, I pray You will help me to overcome any depression and be transformed by the renewing of my mind. (Romans 12:2). Lord, teach me to think on things that are true and to disregard what is false (Philippians 4:8). When I am feeling anxious, help me to be quick to pray, and for You to fill me with Your peace (Philippians 4:6–7). When I am feeling low, call to my mind all the ways You have blessed me in the past. Lord, give me strong faith that You will never leave me or forsake me (Hebrews 13:8). Guard my heart and mind, Lord. Put the right people in my path who know how to help.

Look over the scriptures you studied today and let them guide you as you write your own prayer below that addresses your specific needs.

A PRAYER TO
Overcome Envy

One day as I read the Bible, the Lord spoke to my heart through a verse that says, “For where envy and self-seeking exist, confusion and every evil thing are there” (James 3:16). It was as if the Lord pointed to me and said, “You have confusion in your life right now because of the envy and self-seeking in your heart.”

How embarrassed I felt. Me? Have envy? But I came to realize that constantly measuring myself against others was the seed from which envy grows. This is the lie we believe when we are envious of someone: “I need and deserve to have what he or she has.” The truth is that everything we have comes from God. When we receive a blessing from God we need to be careful not to be boastful or arrogant about it. On the other hand, we are to guard against envy when we see someone who possesses something that we don’t. To have sorrow, discontent, or ill will over someone else’s possessions or advantages is to reject what God is able to give us. The deception of envy is thinking that God doesn’t have enough to go around.

Key Scripture

“Envy is rottenness to the bones” (Proverbs 14:30).

Prepare to Pray

Envy and jealousy go hand in hand. Envy is the ultimate idolatry, and idolatry is the root of envy. The Bible says we are to put to death "covetousness, which is idolatry" (Colossians 3:5) because it will undermine the purposes of God in our lives. Envy will put great limitations on your life. If you are envious of what someone has, you will either never have that yourself, or you will get it and won't be satisfied by it. The Bible asks, "Who is able to stand before jealousy?" (Proverbs 27:4). Whether in you or directed at you, envy is evil. Satan fell from heaven because he wanted what God had. It will be your downfall, too. Focus on making the apostle Paul's attitude your attitude. He said, "For we brought nothing into this world, and it is certain we can carry nothing out. And having food and clothing, with these we shall be content" (1 Timothy 6:7–8).

Study the Scriptures

- Look up and read Galatians 5:16–23. Compare and contrast the works of the flesh compared to the fruit of the Spirit.

- In what areas are you prone to envy? Write them down.

- How would you describe the difference between the "works of the flesh" and "walking in the Spirit"?

- Why do you think it's necessary to rely on the Holy Spirit's power to deal with envy? Practically speaking, what would that look like in your life?

- Look up the following passages and consider how they relate to envy. How can you apply these truths to your own life?

Luke 12:15	
1 Corinthians 3:3	
James 3:14–16	
Philippians 4:8, 11	
Hebrews 13:5–6	

Respond to God's Word

In the book of Galatians, the apostle Paul makes it clear that at any given time we are either defaulting to the works of the flesh or walking in the Spirit (5:16). But remember, unless you are intentional about walking in the power of the Holy Spirit, you will default to the works of your flesh. You might be wondering, *Which one is stronger, the flesh or the Spirit*? It depends on which one you are feeding. If you are giving in to worldly behavior, thoughts, attitudes, and taking your cues from modern culture, you can be certain that you're walking in the flesh. On the other hand, if you are intentional about nurturing your spiritual life by praying, reading God's Word, participating in praise and worship, and being active in biblical community, you'll be much more inclined to walk in the Spirit.

The good news is, if you've fallen into a pattern of walking in the flesh, you can decide today to turn your back on the works of the flesh and fully engage yourself in walking in the Spirit. But remember, this is a decision you'll have to make on a regular basis, because if you fall out of the pattern of walking in the Spirit—you'll default to walking in the flesh, and that's when sins like envy (and a whole other dirty laundry list of things) creep into your life.

Pray the Scriptures

Father, show me any place in me where I have envy, and I will repent from this behavior (1 John 1:9). Help me to always walk in the power of the Holy Spirit and put to death the deeds of the flesh (Romans 8:13). Lord, I thank You for the ways You have uniquely gifted me. I pray I will use what I have to give you glory. Remove anything else in me that is offensive to You. Fill me with the fruits of Your Spirit so my life will be characterized by love, joy, peace, longsuffering, kindness, goodness, faithfulness, and self-control (Galatians 5:22–23). Enable me to become more like You.

Look over the scriptures you studied today and let them guide you as you write your own prayer below that addresses your specific needs.

A PRAYER TO
Overcome Fear

Fear was the controlling factor of my life before I received Jesus: fear of failure, of bodily harm, of being emotionally hurt, of getting old, of being a nobody. An aching, paralyzing, all-engulfing spirit of fear had overtaken me, bringing with it companion spirits of suicide, despair, anxiety, and hopelessness. As I fought to keep from drowning in my fears, I ran out of strength.

I have heard it said many times that F-E-A-R stands for False Evidence Appearing Real. When the devil presents false evidence and makes it seem real, we can choose to listen to his falsehoods or believe God. One of the biggest fears for anyone who has been emotionally neglected or abused as a child is fear of the opinions of others. Our fears tell us, *People won't like me when they find out what I'm really like.* But Isaiah 51:7 tells us, "Do not fear the reproach of men, nor be afraid of their insults." Because of Jesus, we never have to live in fear of the opinions of others.

Key Scripture

"For God has not given us a spirit of fear, but of power and of love and of a sound mind" (2 Timothy 1:7).

Prepare to Pray

The lie we believe when we are afraid is "God is not able to keep me and all that I care about safe." To be sure, there is much to be afraid of in this world, but when the strength of that fear outweighs our sense of God's presence, a spirit of fear can attach itself to our personality. If frightening or traumatizing things have happened to us in childhood, we believe this lie all the more. We think God is not in control of our situation.

The opposite of fear is faith, and we usually interpret the circumstances of our lives through one or the other. Fear causes us to live like we are emotionally paralyzed. We fear not having enough, so we don't give. We fear being hurt, so we hesitate to love. We fear being taken advantage of, so we don't serve others. We fear rejection, so we don't step out and do what God has called us to do.

Study the Scriptures

- Look up and read Psalm 34. What stands out to you in this passage?

- Reread Psalm 34:4–6. What were the results when the psalmist prayed about his fears?

- Being fearful about something differs from an appropriate "fear of the LORD," which means to hold in reverential awe. How would you describe the difference between the two?

- Write down the areas you struggle with fear and find a Scripture passage that speaks to your specific situation. Start praying the Scriptures over your fears.

- Look up the following passages and consider how they relate to fear. How can you apply these truths to your own life?

Deuteronomy 31:6	
Psalm 27:1	
Isaiah 35:3–4	
Isaiah 41:10	
1 John 4:18	

Respond to God's Word

Realizing that fear doesn't come from God and you don't have to live in it is the first step in freeing yourself. Here are a few more things you can do when you are afraid: First, confess your fear to the Lord and ask Him to free you from it. Don't deny your fear. Take it to God instead and pray for deliverance.

Second, check to see if there is, in fact, a very real danger, and do what you can to remedy the situation. Have others pray with you until the danger passes and you have peace about it. Third, commit to trusting the Lord. Identify Scripture passages that speak to your specific fears and commit to praying those passages daily. Lastly, worship the Lord out loud. Praise is your greatest weapon against fear, so use it with great force. Clap your hands, sing, and speak praises to God. Thank Him for His great love. The more you do, the more you'll open up to receive it.

No matter what has happened to you or is happening in the world around you, God promises to protect you as you walk with Him. In fact, He is committed to protecting you all the time. We don't know how much evil the Lord protects us from every day, but I'm sure it's far more than we imagine. He is more powerful than any adversary we face, and He promises that no matter what the Enemy brings into our lives, we will triumph in it. The only fear you are to have is the fear of God, a respect for God's authority and power. Fearing God means fearing what life without Him would be and thanking Him continually that because of His love you'll never have to experience it.

Pray the Scriptures

Father, Your Word makes it clear that You have not given me a spirit of fear, but of power and of love and of a sound mind (2 Timothy 1:7). Jesus, I confess that I am dealing with fear (name specific areas). Lord, You are my light and salvation, and therefore, I know I have no reason to be afraid (Psalm 27:1). I thank You, God, because Your Word promises that You are with me. Therefore, I will not be dismayed, because You are my God. I pray You will strengthen me and help me. Jesus, I pray You will uphold me with Your righteous right hand (Isaiah 41:10).

Look over the scriptures you studied today and let them guide you as you write your own prayer below that addresses your specific needs.

A PRAYER FOR

Dealing with Anger

The Bible has plenty to say about anger, but it does not say we should never get angry. The Scriptures set two limits on our anger. First, we must not hurt someone verbally or physically. Second, we should take our anger to God quickly and not carry it around inside us so that we sin. The lie we believe when we have frequent outbursts of anger is, "My rights are most important, and if they are violated, I am fully justified in being angry." The deception of anger is believing we have a right to be angry at anyone but the devil. People and situations that make us angry are actually pawns Satan uses against us.

Key Scripture

"'Be angry, and do not sin;' do not let the sun go down on your wrath, nor give place to the devil" (Ephesians 4:26-27).

Prepare to Pray

After I was healed of deep-rooted unforgiveness toward my mother, I still had to deal with recurring anger toward her because of her verbal abuse every time I was with her. "The devil is using your mother to attack you, Stormie," my counselor explained when I went to her office for help. "She is a willing vessel because she is controlled by those spirits. Your war is with Satan, not her."

Learning to be angry with the devil and not my mother was extremely difficult, especially when I was in her presence. I constantly had to remind myself who my enemy really was, but the lines of distinction became quickly blurred. Eventually I was able to get rid of anger when I wasn't around her, but she died before I could master it when we were together. Every time I was with her, I had to confess my anger to God and ask Him to help me.

Study the Scriptures

- Look up and read Proverbs 22:24–25. What are the risks of being friends with angry people?

- Look up and read Proverbs 29:22. What are two characteristics of a habitually angry person?

- Everyone gets angry on occasion, but for some, anger is a serious problem that's turned into chronic sin. How do you deal with anger?

- What types of things tend to make you angry?

❁ **Look up the following passages and consider how they relate to anger. How can you apply these truths to your own life?**

Psalm 37:7–8	
Proverbs 14:16–17	
Proverbs 15:1–3	
Proverbs 16:32	
Proverbs 29:11	

Respond to God's Word

Whenever we become angry, we have options as to how we will express that anger. Think about how you handle your anger and check the ways that apply to you:

- ☐ I often suppress my anger.
- ☐ I give the person the silent treatment.

- ☐ I tend to be openly aggressive. Sometimes I let my anger explode into harsh words.
- ☐ Sometimes I strike out against the person.
- ☐ Sometimes I try to be calmly assertive. I try to state my opinion without emotion and as reasonably as possible.
- ☐ Sometimes I let go of my anger.

The problem with anger, as with all the other deceptions, is that if it is not dealt with properly before the Lord, it will become a spirit of anger, which will control your life. If you are susceptible to sudden angry outbursts or if your anger level outweighs the offense and is repeated and uncontrollable, then you may have a spirit of anger. It can be inherited from a parent or picked up from observing parental outbursts when you were a child. Or if you were the victim of someone else's anger, your own unforgiveness or inability to release that memory can cause you to react violently now. I've found that anger usually has more to do with people's hurt than it does their hate.

The Bible says, "Let all bitterness, wrath, anger, clamor, and evil speaking be put away from you, with all malice. And be kind to one another, tenderhearted, forgiving one another, even as God in Christ forgave you" (Ephesians 4:31–32). It also says if we don't do that, we grieve the Holy Spirit. You will never find peace, restoration, and wholeness if you nurture a spirit of anger. Every single angry outburst will be a step backward from where you want to go or be, and it will keep your prayers from being answered. The wisest thing you can do is pray about your anger. Tell God why you are angry. You might even feel inclined to "tell on people," and that's OK to do. God invites you to cast all of your cares on Him, and that includes things you are angry about (1 Peter 5:6–7).

Pray the Scriptures

Father, I confess I am angry about (name specific reason). Lord, I do not want to sin. So I ask You to give me Your perspective about the way I am feeling and wisdom regarding this situation (James 1:5). I especially pray that You will help me control my speech when I'm angry (Ephesians 4:29). Also, give me Your perspective about when I need to speak up and when to stay quiet. Jesus, I pray You will enable me to release my anger. Show me how to proceed in peace and wisdom. Lord, I hand my anger over to You, asking that You will show me how to move forward without it.

Look over the scriptures you studied today and let them guide you as you write your own prayer below that addresses your specific needs.

A PRAYER TO
Overcome Pride

Oddly enough, pride is one of the biggest problems for someone who has been emotionally abused or neglected. It's hard to spot because it is so hidden inside and covered with feelings of low self-worth. I always believed I didn't have pride. In fact, I took pride in that. But it wasn't true. When I was working as a television entertainer, I feared failure even more than I desired success. This fear of failure was not humility, but pride. I felt I deserved to be successful. But my pride made me all the more susceptible to failure. The lie we believe when we are prideful is, *I'm in control of my life, I'm important, and I can make things happen the way I want them to happen.* The opposite—humility—says, "Without God I am nothing, but I can do all things through Christ who strengthens me" (Philippians 4:13).

Keep in mind, humility doesn't mean you think poorly of yourself. It simply means that you realize that apart from God you are destined for sin and destruction. Romans 3:23 says, "For all have sinned and fall short of the glory of God." Part of being humble means acknowledging that there is an all-powerful and perfect God—and you and I are not Him.

Key Scripture

"Everyone proud in heart is an abomination to the LORD" (Proverbs 16:5).

Prepare to Pray

The deception of pride is thinking that our will is more important than God's will. This was Satan's downfall. He didn't want to let God be God and do things God's way. His last words before he was cast out of heaven were "I will exalt my throne above the stars of God" (Isaiah 14:13). When we think our way is the better way or question God's will for our lives, we are acting in pride. God knows the whole story from beginning to end. God knows things we don't, He has information we lack, and He understands things we have no concept of. To pretend to believe we know better than God is not only foolish—it is the sin of pride. Pride is a costly sin that has inevitable consequences. The writer of Proverbs said, "A man's pride will bring him low, but the humble in spirit will retain honor" (29:23). The key to dealing with pride is confessing it in prayer and humbling ourselves before God.

Study the Scriptures

- Look up and read James 4:1–10. What does this passage reveal regarding the topic of pride?

- What are some of the negative consequences of pride according to this passage?

- Glance back and reread James 4:6. How does God respond to the prideful? How does He respond to the humble?

- Write down any areas where you struggle with pride. What consequences have you experienced as a result of pride? Are there areas you need to confess your pride to God? Ask Him, if you don't know.

- Look up the following passages and consider how they relate to pride. How can you apply these truths to your own life?

2 Chronicles 12:6–7	
Proverbs 16:5	
Proverbs 16:18	
Proverbs 28:25	
Proverbs 29:23	

Respond to God's Word

Pride comes from being afraid that you have no value as a person. It says, "I have to be great because I fear I'll be nothing." At the opposite extreme is the thought, *If I can't be the best, then I'll be the worst. If I can't make people love me, then I'll make them hate me.* Prisons are crowded with people who have felt that way. The more spiritually mature we become, the more we see that without God we are nothing. It is He who gives us our worth: "For if anyone thinks himself to be something, when he is nothing, he deceives himself" (Galatians 6:3).

The writer of Proverbs advises us, "Do not be wise in your own eyes; fear the LORD and depart from evil. It will be health to your flesh, and strength to your bones" (3:7–8). It takes a lot of healing to come from feeling like a nothing to accepting your worth in Jesus, then to admitting that apart from God you are nothing. But when you can do that, it will be God in you that leads you to greatness. And when great things happen in your life it will be obvious to you that God's grace (rather than your own merit) allowed for those great things to happen. Ask God to give you a humble heart.

Pray the Scriptures

Father, Your Word says You resist the proud but give grace to the humble (James 4:6). Lord, I don't want You to resist me in any way. I want to please You in every area of my life. I confess the sin of pride in (list specific area). I confess this behavior and attitude as sin and ask for Your forgiveness in Jesus' name (1 John 1:9). God, I submit myself to You and Your will for my life. I know You know best as to how my life should go. I pray You will help me resist the

devil so he will flee from me. Father, I humble myself before You and ask for Your grace to help me.

Look over the scriptures you studied today and let them guide you as you write your own prayer below that addresses your specific needs.

A PRAYER TO
Overcome Spiritual Laziness

Apart from God, we all walk in rebellion. But rebellion can happen in us even after we've trusted Jesus as our Savior and are living in obedience. In fact, we can fall into rebellion without even realizing it. One of the most common forms of rebellion among believers is spiritual laziness. We all know if we've just robbed a liquor store, murdered someone, or committed adultery. We're not as keen at recognizing when we have drifted away from the mainstream of God's Spirit in our lives.

Key Scripture

"But I am afraid that just as Eve was deceived by the serpent's cunning, your minds may somehow be led astray from your sincere and pure devotion to Christ" (2 Corinthians 11:3 NIV).

Prepare to Pray

The danger once we know Jesus and have been walking His way is thinking that we have learned the lessons. We've read the Bible. We're receiving the blessings. And now we believe we can let things slide. We become lazy in what we have already learned to do. We let church attendance become a lower priority, allow our giving to slack off, and look the other way when certain steps of obedience fall by the wayside—while the Enemy sneaks up on our blind side. Too many battles have been lost by just this sort of rebellion. Trusting Christ as our Savior is a one-time decision, but continuing to walk in daily obedience to Him is a decision we'll need to make every day of our life. Jesus told His disciples, "If anyone desires to come after Me, let him deny himself, and take up his cross daily, and follow Me" (Luke 9:23).

Study the Scriptures

- Look up and read Philippians 1:9–11. What kinds of things did Paul pray for the church at Philippi?

- Paul's epistles often began with a prayer for spiritual strength for those he was writing the letter to. Why is it wise to pray for your own spiritual life?

- What types of things do you most often pray for? How can you expand on that by including prayers for spiritual strength and growth?

- Look up and read Psalm 51:12. What did King David request? How can you use his prayer to guide your own prayer life?

- Look up the following passages and consider how they relate to rebellion and spiritual laziness. How can you apply these truths to your own life?

Nehemiah 9:26–27	
Isaiah 1:19–20	
Psalm 5:10–12	
Psalm 107:10–14	

Respond to God's Word

If you take a close look at the apostle Paul's prayers recorded in Scripture, you'll notice Paul always prioritized praying for spiritual strength and flourishing. God invites us to take all of our cares to Him in prayer and that should include prayers for our spiritual life. There's nothing wrong with praying for things like job interviews to go well, mortgages to be approved, and good test results at the doctor's office, but you are cutting yourself short if you limit your prayers to those types of requests. If you have fallen into a pattern of rebellion or spiritual apathy, it's imperative that you pray for your spiritual life. And even if you aren't in a season of spiritual apathy right now, it's wise to pray you don't fall into that trap.

Do you wonder if you are falling into rebellion by drifting spiritually? A number of warning signs can help you prevent such a fall. Periodically check the following statements to see if any apply to you:

- I am allowing outer sources like social media, online influencers, TV, movies, and books to mold me more than the Holy Spirit does.
- I'm influenced more by what my friends say than by what God is telling me through His Word.
- I am becoming spiritually malnourished because I am not daily feeding on the Word of God or feasting in His presence in prayer and praise.
- I am beginning to think I've heard it all, so I have no reason to go to church or Bible study.
- I've begun to do a few things I formerly avoided, ignoring what I've learned to be right, in favor of a new experience.
- I've begun to make decisions without godly counsel because it feels right.
- I haven't asked the Lord specifically about a major purchase, but it's something I've always wanted, so it must be God's will.
- I haven't done anything wrong, so I don't need to ask God to reveal any unconfessed sin.

If any of the above statements ring true for you, take it before the Lord in repentance immediately so that you can be taken off the path that leads to destruction. There's nothing more important than your relationship with Jesus.

Pray the Scriptures

Jesus, above all things I pray I will always love You with all my heart, soul, mind, and strength (Mark 12:30). Let my love for You grow with ever increasing measure. Lord, I pray nothing will ever threaten my love and pure devotion for You (2 Corinthians 11:3). Guard me from distraction and the schemes of the Enemy. Remove any hint of rebellion and spiritual apathy in me. Teach me to love the things You love and hate the things You hate. I pray I will be strong in You and in the power of Your might (Ephesians 6:10).

Look over the scriptures you studied today and let them guide you as you write your own prayer below that addresses your specific needs.

A PRAYER TO
Heal from Rejection

My earliest memory of rejection is of being locked in a closet by my mother. Had it been an isolated incident, it might not have been so bad. But it wasn't. As a result, I grew up feeling rejected, and the feelings of rejection grew in me until no amount of affirmation and encouragement could overcome them. I became an overachiever to gain approval. I worked hard so that people would notice me and say I did a good job. When they did, the good feeling only lasted for the moment. I was certain that if people really knew the truth about me and my limitations, they would not have such a favorable opinion. I expected rejection. But after I became a Christian, I learned that it's not God's will for His children to continue in patterns of defeat. Maybe you can relate. If you're struggling with the impact of rejection, be encouraged, because it's God's will for you to overcome rejection.

Key Scripture

"The LORD has appeared of old to me, saying: 'Yes, I have loved you with an everlasting love; therefore with lovingkindness I have drawn you'" (Jeremiah 31:3).

Prepare to Pray

The lie we believe when we feel rejection is, *I'm not worth anything, so it's completely understandable that people will reject me.* A spirit of rejection convinces you that you will be rejected, and then every word and action of other people is interpreted through the eyes of rejection. Each of us has been rejected—by a family member, a friend, a teacher, a stranger, or a casual acquaintance. When we're emotionally healthy, such an incident won't set us back much. We are soon able to put it in perspective and get over it.

But if we have deep emotional scars from repeated incidents of rejection, the smallest incident will feel like a knife to the heart. But the good news is, that if you belong to Jesus Christ there is no reason for you to continue to suffer with rejection. When you begin to understand the truth about your identity in Christ, you'll know you are truly accepted, embraced, and loved by the God who chose you. Regardless of what other people say or do, if you are a Christian, your identify is found in Christ. And what the Bible says about you is the truth you live by.

Study the Scriptures

- Look up and read Hebrews 13:5. How does knowing God will never leave you or forsake you impact your feelings about rejection?

- Look up and read Psalm 23:5 and visualize God preparing a table for you in the presence of your enemies and inviting you to take your seat. How does knowing you have a place where you are welcome at God's table influence your thoughts about rejection?

- Look up and read Psalm 27:10. What does this passage say about being rejected by family?

- Write down the people and situations that have caused you to feel rejected. Use this list as a prayer guide and ask God to fill the voids where you feel rejected. Look up Scripture passages that speak directly to your feelings of rejection.

- Look up the following passages and consider how they relate to rejection. How can you apply these truths to your own life?

Deuteronomy 7:6	
1 Samuel 12:22	

Isaiah 41:9–10	
Psalm 94:12–15	
Hebrews 13:5–6	

Respond to God's Word

The best way to confront a spirit of rejection is to fill yourself with the knowledge of God's acceptance. Find all the verses in the Bible about God's acceptance and compile a list. As you read, study, and pray these verses you'll develop a much deeper understanding of God's love and how to receive it. God said, "I chose you out of the world" (John 15:19). We did not choose Jesus first; He chose us. We must learn to live like the chosen ones we are.

When you sense the red light of rejection flashing off and on in your brain over some word or action someone has said or done, remember that Jesus chose you. Remember, too, that the voice of God always encourages; the voice of the devil always discourages. If you can't see anything good about yourself, it's because the devil has covered up your future with the past. Keep in mind, there will be times when people disappoint you and you'll feel the sting of rejection. But when you are convinced of God's love and acceptance you'll be able to move forward knowing that no matter what—you are loved, wanted, and well cared for in Christ.

Pray the Scriptures

Dear Lord, I have felt the pain of rejection (name specific circumstance). God, I know it is not Your will for me to live with feelings of chronic rejection. I thank You because Your Word promises that You will never leave or forsake me (Hebrews 13:5). Even when other people disappoint me, I know that You will always do what is best for me. Even if other people do reject me, I know that You have chosen me (John 15:19). Jesus, help me to remember that You love me so much You gave Your life for me (John 3:16). I pray Your everlasting love will help me overcome my feelings of rejection.

Look over the scriptures you studied today and let them guide you as you write your own prayer below that addresses your specific needs.

A PRAYER TO
Overcome Self-Pity

Self-pity is a recipe for misery. If we're not careful, it's possible to fall into the trap of being negatively self-focused. The lie that plays over and over in our mind is, *Poor me. The worst things always happen to me.* It's important to weed out any habits related to self-pity. God disapproves of self-pity, and other people don't enjoy being around someone filled with self-pity.

Refusing to dwell in self-pity doesn't mean that you don't acknowledge that hard things have happened to you. But as a believer, you have the opportunity to have God touch the places where you have wounds, to heal from things that have happened in the past, and to move forward in thanksgiving because Jesus has changed your life and rewritten your future.

Self-pity is a work of the devil, who is intent upon stealing life away from you to destroy you. Remember that. It may seem right to be sorry for yourself because of bad things that have happened, but allowing yourself to feel that way all the time means you are ignoring the power of God in your life now. And that's exactly what Satan wants. Self-pity keeps you forever from moving into all God has for you.

Key Scripture

"But you, beloved, building yourselves up on your most holy faith, praying in the Holy Spirit, keep yourselves in the love of God, looking for the mercy of our Lord Jesus Christ unto eternal life" (Jude 20–21).

Prepare to Pray

Self-pity keeps us focused entirely on ourselves. The opposite of focusing inward on self is focusing outward on God. We mistakenly think that an intense focus on ourselves will contribute most to our happiness and fulfillment, when actually the opposite is true.

Dwelling on ourselves leads to emotional sickness. Instead of being filled with thoughts about what we need and feel, we must be full of thoughts of the Lord. Our complete focus must be on God alone. The Bible says, "The backslider in heart will be filled with his own ways, but a good man will be satisfied from above" (Proverbs 14:14). The best way to focus on God is to thank Him continually for all He has given, praise Him for all He has done, and worship Him for all He is.

Study the Scriptures

- Look up and read Psalm 107:8. How can giving thanks to God for all the ways He has blessed you shift your focus from self-pity to joy?

- In what areas are you prone to self-pity? What evidence do you see that God has been faithful to you even in the most difficult aspects of your life? How can you turn those "difficult aspects of life" into praise to God?

- Look up and read 1 Thessalonians 5:17–18. According to this passage, what is God's will for you?

- Write down a list of several things you are thankful for. Get in the habit of writing down five or more new things each day.

❁ **Look up the following passages and consider how they relate to self-pity. How can you apply these truths to your own life?**

Proverbs 25:28	
2 Corinthians 7:9–11	
2 Corinthians 13:4–6	
Galatians 2:20	
Jude 20–21	

Respond to God's Word

It's impossible to be self-focused with self-pity while you are glorifying God. Also, resolve that you will not sin with your mind or your mouth. Say aloud, "I refuse to sit around thinking about what I need and want and feel. I refuse to mourn and moan about the past, present, and future. I deliberately choose to think about only You, Lord, and Your goodness. I look to You to meet all my needs. You know what they are even better than I do." Deliberately avoid the pitfall of self-pity by focusing on the Lord in thanksgiving and praise to your Creator. Your emotional health depends on it.

Pray the Scriptures

Heavenly Father, I confess that I have fallen into the trap of self-pity (name specific areas). I confess self-pity as sin and ask for Your forgiveness in Jesus' name (1 John 1:9). Lord, I want to be mindful of the fact that what You have done for me is far greater than any bad thing that has ever happened to me. You have given me reason to praise You every day of my life. I give thanks for (name specific blessings). Jesus, I pray You will help me overcome any tendencies toward self-pity. Help me to see Your blessings and give You thanks all the days of my life. I do not want to be known for complaining—I want to be known for praising You and giving thanks to Your holy and precious name.

Look over the scriptures you studied today and let them guide you as you write your own prayer below that addresses your specific needs.

A PRAYER TO
Stand Strong During Spiritual Warfare

Spiritual warfare is a topic some believers know little about even though the Enemy attacks all Christians. Oftentimes, spiritual warfare comes on suddenly. Perhaps you are doing everything you know to do, and things are going well, and then suddenly depression clouds your mind, you're overcome with fear and anxiety, or low self-esteem dominates your actions. Or maybe unforgiveness returns in full force, and all hell breaks loose in a relationship. Suddenly, it seems like things are worse than they have ever been. These types of scenarios might mean that you are dealing with spiritual warfare. Don't be frightened; knowing how to respond makes a world of difference.

Key Scripture

"Put on the whole armor of God, that you may be able to stand against the wiles of the devil" (Ephesians 6:11).

Prepare to Pray

In times of spiritual warfare, you have to understand without a doubt that when you walk with Jesus, you never walk backward. God has made it clear in His Word that if we have our eyes on Him, we will go from glory to glory and strength to strength. The apostle Paul told the Corinthians, "But we all, with unveiled face, beholding as in a mirror the glory of the Lord, are being transformed into the same image from glory to glory, just as by the Spirit of the Lord" (2 Corinthians 3:18). And the psalmist tells us, "They go from strength to strength; each one appears before God in Zion" (Psalm 84:7).

To go backward, you would have to deliberately turn your back on God and walk in the other direction. As long as you are looking to Him, you are moving forward. It does not matter how it feels; that's the way it is. Don't get confused. God is on your side. Satan is your enemy and wants you to believe his lies. He comes to you at your weakest (especially physically) and mixes his lies with just enough truth that you believe them. But the Bible isn't silent about how to respond in times of spiritual warfare.

Study the Scriptures

- Look up and read Ephesians 6:10–20. What is the armor of God that Paul describes in these verses?

- Glance back at Ephesians 6:17–18. What role does God's Word and prayer have in spiritual warfare?

- Based on what you read in Ephesians 6:17–18, why do you think it's important to get in the habit of praying the Scriptures?

- In what ways have you experienced spiritual warfare in your own life? Write down three to four Scriptures to pray during times of spiritual warfare.

- Look up the following passages and consider how they relate to spiritual warfare. How can you apply these truths to your own life?

Psalm 18:17	
Proverbs 10:25	
2 Timothy 2:24–26	

James 1:12	
1 Peter 5:8–9	

Respond to God's Word

You might be wondering, *How do I know when I am dealing with spiritual warfare*? After all, sometimes hard things just happen in life, or what you are going through might be part of God's plan for you on your path to becoming a mature believer. When God is working in your life, things that you are attached to are being shaken loose, and parts of your flesh are being crucified. This doesn't feel good. But neither does the attack of the Enemy. The only way you can know for sure which is happening is to let the Spirit of God reveal it to you through His Word. You do that by spending time in His presence in praise and worship and prayer. Say, "Is this You, God, or is this the devil?" He will show you.

Too many people assume that they deserve everything that's happening to them. They don't suspect that what they are experiencing might be a shot directed at them from enemy territory. Often the attack is of such magnitude that we can hardly see straight, let alone figure out clear direction for ourselves. That's why it's important to know how to identify the Enemy's attack and know how to respond. Spiritual warfare is intense and not something you have to attempt to manage alone. But Jesus' strength and power is greater than any spiritual warfare you will ever experience. The apostle John wrote, "You are of God, little children, and have overcome them, because He who is in you is greater than he who is in the world" (1 John 4:4).

Pray the Scriptures

Jesus, You faced the Enemy and already won the battle. I pray You will give me discernment so I know when I am experiencing spiritual warfare. I ask that You deliver me from every evil work (2 Timothy 4:18). Teach me to be strong in You and the power of Your might (Ephesians 6:10). I pray that I will not fear because I know You are with me. Help me not to be dismayed, because You are my God. Give me strength and help me. Hold me up with Your righteous right hand (Isaiah 41:10). God, I know You are faithful and I ask You to guard me against the evil one (2 Thessalonians 3:3). You are my rock and my shield. I take refuge in You. Lord, I call upon You and ask You to save me from my enemies (Psalm 138:7).

Look over the scriptures you studied today and let them guide you as you write your own prayer below that addresses your specific needs.

A PRAYER FOR

When You Are Waiting for Your Prayer to Be Answered

There will be times that your prayers will not be answered—at least not exactly the way you prayed them or according to your timetable. We all have lived through the painful consequences of unanswered prayer. Sometimes what seems like unanswered prayer is actually a matter of waiting on God. Other times the prayers are answered so differently from what we expected that we can't even see they've been answered until much later. Sometimes our prayers are never answered at all as we have prayed them. The key is standing strong in the Lord whether we see that our prayers are answered or not.

When getting an answer to prayer takes a long time, we sometimes lose hope. We become discouraged and fear God has forgotten us. We stop praying, stop going to church, stop reading the Bible, stop obeying God's rules because we think, *What's the point*? Sometimes we get mad at God. We don't like waiting the two weeks, two months, two years, or as long as it takes for the answer to come. But the truth is, we all go through seasons of waiting on God. But even when things don't seem to be happening, you can be sure God is working in you.

Key Scripture

"And we know that all things work together for good to those who love God, to those who are the called according to His purpose" (Romans 8:28).

Prepare to Pray

When you feel your prayers are not answered, God reveals two things to you: His grace and His power. His grace sustains and keeps you, and His power delivers you. God wants us to see without a doubt that we are limited in our power. He also wants us to see that He is not. He sometimes waits until all hope outside of Him is dead so that we will know it is He who brought life where there was none. Sometimes He takes things out of our lives so that we will turn to Him to supply our need. No matter how much God blesses us, He wants us to acknowledge that we depend on Him. And sometimes He uses the storms of our lives to accomplish that purpose.

Study the Scriptures

- Look up and read Matthew 7:7–12. Write down three to four things these verses tell you about prayer.

- Some translations read, "Keep asking, keep seeking, keep knocking." Why is it important to persist in prayer for as long as it takes?

- **Glance back and reread Matthew 7:11. How does this verse communicate that God knows the best things to give to His children?**

- **Do you have prayer requests that you've been waiting for a long time for God to answer? Have you stopped praying about these things? If so, write them down and start praying about them again, if still applicable.**

- **Look up the following passages and consider how they relate to waiting for your prayers to be answered. How can you apply these truths to your own life?**

Isaiah 40:31	
1 Peter 1:6–7	
1 Peter 4:12–13	
1 Peter 5:10	

Respond to God's Word

When you are waiting on God to answer your prayers, be sure you allow no situation to make you turn your back on Him. Know that He sees where you are, He has not forgotten you, and He will sustain you through it. Rest in the fact that He is in control and more powerful than your problems. It's at this time that we can either turn away from God's ways or determine to live by them even more diligently.

Part of standing strong in times of unanswered prayer is waiting, and waiting produces patience. The Bible says, "By your patience possess your souls" (Luke 21:19). When you are patient, you're able to take control of your very being and place yourself in God's hands. He, then, is in control whether it is night or day in your soul. He becomes God to you in every season of your life—the good and the bad. And because you know Him that way, you become unshakable.

Since we have no choice but to wait, our attitude makes a lot of difference. We can either shake our fist at God and scream, "Why me?" Or we can open up our hearts to God and pray, "Lord, change this situation. Perfect Your life in me as I wait on You. Help me to do the right thing, and let it all work out for my greatest good."

Pray the Scriptures

Lord, I praise You as I wait for You to answer my prayers. I confess I'm afraid that my prayers may never be answered. I'm weary and discouraged from the waiting, and feel I'm losing the strength to fight. Forgive me, Lord, for not trusting You more (1 John 1:9). Give me the endurance to keep asking for as long as I need to (Matthew 7:7). Lord, as I wait I pray You will continue to do a good work in me. Your Word says all things work for the good for those who love God (Romans 8:28). I do love You, Lord, and I thank You that in this hard situation You are bringing good things that I may not even see yet. I pray my weariness would end and there would be renewed hope in my spirit. Help me to feel Your presence and Your love, and help me to hear Your voice and follow Your lead. Thank You that You are in full control.

Look over the scriptures you studied today and let them guide you as you write your own prayer below that addresses your specific needs.

A PRAYER TO

Understand Your Identity in Christ

Many of us struggle with feelings of low self-worth, and if you come from a background of verbal abuse, it's even more challenging. *You're never going to amount to anything! You're worthless! You're nothing! You're stupid! You're a failure!* were words my mother used to say to me over and over again. They were reinforced by her lack of affection and inability to nurture. Because we lived on a ranch miles from anyone, I didn't have the positive reinforcement of friends or relatives, which could have lessened the impact of my mother's neglect. Every day I heard the same words, and I grew up believing them.

Since I believed I was nobody, I became desperate to prove I was somebody. I grabbed for things instead of letting them happen. I demanded approval. I had to be noticed. Starved for love, I became involved in one destructive relationship after another. Yet no amount of love, approval, or recognition ever filled the endless void of my being, because I believed those lies about myself.

Key Scripture

"For we know, brothers and sisters loved by God, that he has chosen you" (1 Thessalonians 1:4 NIV).

Prepare to Pray

We all want to be somebody. The truth is, God created each one of us to be somebody and no life is an accident or unwanted in His eyes. He has given us each a distinct purpose or calling. It is not humility to deny the Lord's extraordinary qualities in us; it's low self-esteem. High self-esteem means seeing yourself as God sees you and recognizing that you are a unique person in whom He has placed specific gifts, talents, and purpose unlike anyone else. Memorize today's Key Scripture and say it aloud fifty times a day if you need to. Do whatever it takes to help you remember it. This is the absolute truth about you, whether you can see it or not and whether or not anyone else recognizes it.

Study the Scriptures

- Look up the following verses and write down how the Bible describes you.

2 Corinthians 5:17	
Ephesians 2:10	
2 Timothy 1:7	

John 1:12	
1 Thessalonians 1:2–4	

- What new insight did you gain from the Scriptures above?

- What falsehoods do you tend to believe about yourself? Where do these thoughts originate?

- What specific Scriptures do you need to rely on (memorize, pray, ponder) when you are struggling with untrue thoughts about yourself?

- Look up the following passages and consider how they relate to your identity in Christ. How can you apply these truths to your own life?

Psalm 139:14	
Romans 8:37–39	

Galatians 2:20	
Ephesians 1:7	

Respond to God's Word

No matter what anyone says, God gets the last word about you. He has gone to great lengths to reveal your identity in Christ on the pages of Holy Scripture. As a Christian, it's your responsibility to know what God's Word says about you and to believe it. The scriptures listed above are just the starting point—the Bible has many more passages that teach believers who they are in Christ Jesus. I have learned to value myself as God values me by deliberately thanking Him for any positive things I see.

As we praise God for specific things, we are inviting His presence to bring transformation. It's the best medicine I know for believing lies about yourself. The Bible says, "A house divided against itself will fall" (Luke 11:17 NIV). This means that a person who has turned against herself won't make it. For better or worse, we live out what we believe to be true about ourselves. Much of your emotional pain may be caused by believing untrue things about yourself. If you entertain lies about yourself, or if you question your identity in Christ, it's imperative you learn what the Bible says about you. Ponder what it says, ask God to confirm these truths in your mind and heart, and help you to live these truths out in your life.

Pray the Scriptures

Lord, I pray that by Your power I will understand my identity in Christ. Help me to always remember that I am Your daughter (John 1:12). Because of Jesus, my past is forgiven, and my future is secure (Ephesians 1:7). I thank You because You have given me skills and talents and You call me to use my gifts to glorify You. I don't need to worry because You make me competent to do everything You call me to do (2 Corinthians 3:5–6). I thank You because I am loved, I am embraced, and You will never leave or forsake me. Because You are with me, there is no reason for me to fear. Thank You for giving me a spirit of love and a sound mind (2 Timothy 1:7). Lord, I confess I am prone to forget who I am and sometimes I fall into the trap of believing lies about myself. Make me quick to redirect my thoughts to Your Word and remind myself of who I am in Christ.

Look over the scriptures you studied today and let them guide you as you write your own prayer below that addresses your specific needs.

A PRAYER TO
Grow Up in the Lord

When it comes to our faith, being on the fence is a sign of indecisiveness and immaturity. If we are going to be mature believers in Jesus Christ, there comes a time when we have to stand up and say, "This is what I believe; this is the way I will live; this is what I will and will not accept—and that's the way it is." We have to decide to stand strong and do what we know is right to do no matter what happens around us.

The Bible doesn't say we won't have problems. In fact, it says quite the opposite: "Many are the afflictions of the righteous, but the LORD delivers him out of them all" (Psalm 34:19). We don't need to fear because God uses our problems for good when we commit them to prayer and are obedient to His ways. Bad things do happen to good people. God never said they wouldn't. He didn't say life is fair. He said He is fair, and He will bring life out of our problems. Jesus actually warned that we would experience problems.

Key Scripture

"These things I have spoken to you, that in Me you may have peace. In the world you will have tribulation; but be of good cheer, I have overcome the world" (John 16:33).

Prepare to Pray

One of the last times I saw my counselor before she moved away, I went to her for some problem that I don't even remember now. What I do remember was her wise counsel, which amounted to two words: "Grow up," she said lovingly.

"What?" I asked.

"It's time to grow up, Stormie," she repeated in her patient voice.

"Grow up?" I repeated, hoping for more details.

"Yes, Stormie. You need to get alone with the Lord and ask Him the questions you're asking me. Then you tell me what He's saying to you."

A point comes in our walk with the Lord when we've had enough teaching, enough counseling, enough deliverance, and enough knowledge of God's ways to be able to stand on our own two feet and say, "I am not going to live on the negative side of life anymore."

Study the Scriptures

- Look up and read 1 Corinthians 3:1–3. When Paul spoke of "milk" and "solid food," he was referring to elementary Bible teachings versus advanced teaching for more mature believers. Why is it important to continue to mature in God's Word so you can receive "solid food" and not remain a babe in Christ?

- Glance back at 1 Corinthians 3:3. What evidence did Paul give that revealed why the Corinthians were still immature?

- Think for a moment about your own spiritual life. Would you describe yourself as a "babe in Christ" or a more mature believer?

- What steps do you need to take to continue to grow in wisdom and understanding of God's Word?

- Look up the following passages and consider how they relate to growing up and maturing in Christ. How can you apply these truths to your own life?

1 Corinthians 13:11	
2 Timothy 2:15	

Hebrews 5:13–14	
Hebrews 6:1	

Respond to God's Word

When we first become a Christian, we are all "babes in Christ." Becoming a mature Christian is a process that doesn't happen overnight, and if you are a new Christian, you should expect it will take some time to grow. But some people fall into the trap of being a believer for decades and never maturing or growing. They don't commit to the spiritual practices of Bible reading and prayer. And then when hard times come, they don't know how to move forward.

We can't depend on someone to hold our hand and make difficult times go away. We have to "grow up" and take responsibility for our lives. We have to decide we won't be the victims of our circumstances, because God has given us a way out. We are not to stand in our own power. We must stand strong in Him. "Let the weak say, 'I am strong,'" the Bible says (Joel 3:10). This does not mean you say, "I think I can" or "Maybe I'll try." You say, "This is it. I will stand firm in the Lord. I will stand strong against the Enemy. I will not cry, complain, and lament over what isn't. I will rejoice over what is and all that God is doing, and will do in the future."

Pray the Scriptures

Lord, I want to be like Jesus, who "increased in wisdom and stature, and in favor with God and men" (Luke 2:52). I pray the Father of glory will give me the spirit of wisdom and revelation in the knowledge of You (Ephesians 1:17). Jesus, help me to "grow up" in every area of my life. I pray the Holy Spirit will convict me of areas where I need to mature. Lord, I pray You will remove everything in my character that You find offensive and in its place I ask You to fill me with the fruit of the Spirit, which are love, joy, peace, patience, kindness, goodness, faithfulness, gentleness, and self-control (Galatians 5:22–23 ESV).

Look over the scriptures you studied today and let them guide you as you write your own prayer below that addresses your specific needs.

A PRAYER FOR

A Growing Understanding of God's Grace

God's grace disrupts our natural way of thinking. Human beings tend to think in terms of *If you do this for me, then I'll do that for you.* And we don't like to be in debt to anyone. When we exchange gifts, we prefer our gift-giving to be equal in nature. It's embarrassing to receive a "big gift" when we've given a smaller one. But God doesn't think like humans, and the greatest example of God's grace was displayed on the cross. I spent years learning to understand what was accomplished on the cross, and it simply means that Jesus took all that I have coming to me—pain, sickness, failure, confusion, hatred, rejection, and death—and gave me all that He had coming to Him—all His wholeness, healing, love, acceptance, peace, joy, and life. Because of God's grace, all we have to do is say, "Jesus, come live in me and be Lord over my life." Our salvation is an act of God's grace because not a single one of us deserves Christ's salvation. But God's grace doesn't stop at the cross—He gives us the grace we need in every area of our lives.

Key Scripture

"For by grace you have been saved through faith, and that not of yourselves; it is the gift of God, not of works, lest anyone should boast" (Ephesians 2:8–9).

Prepare to Pray

A story to illustrate God's grace: In my early twenties my lifestyle was motivated by a desperate need for love. Among the disastrous by-products of this lifestyle were two abortions in less than two years. Both were ugly, frightening, and physically and emotionally traumatic (not to mention illegal at the time), yet I felt relief more than remorse about them. Only after I began to walk with the Lord and learn of His ways did I see what I had done.

When Michael and I decided to have a baby, month after month went by and I didn't get pregnant. I, who had gotten pregnant so easily before, thought surely I was being punished for the abortions. *God, I know I don't deserve to give birth to new life after twice destroying life within me*, I prayed. *I deserve to be childless. But please have mercy and help me to conceive.*

He answered that prayer, and my children have been the greatest example of God's mercy and grace to me. He gave me exactly what I did not deserve. God's grace is for those who live in His kingdom and who allow His kingdom to live in them. We can't receive His grace unless we receive Him. It's a gift that is with Him in His hand. Once we accept Him, He accepts us and refrains from punishing us as we deserve.

Study the Scriptures

- Look up and read John 1:17. According to this passage, where does grace originate?

- Pause for a moment and think about the sacrifice Jesus made for you when He died on the cross for your sins and rose from the dead. In your own words, describe why the cross was the ultimate act of grace.

- Look up and read Romans 6:1–2. How do these verses speak to the notion that you can do whatever you want because God's grace will cover it?

- Write down a few of the ways God has shown you grace. Be specific and include these things in today's prayer and give thanks to God for them.

- Look up the following passages and consider how they relate to God's grace. How can you apply these truths to your own life?

Proverbs 3:34	
Matthew 5:7	

Romans 9:16	
2 Corinthians 12:9	
Ephesians 2:8–9	

Respond to God's Word

Grace is from God. He does it. Not us. Grace is always a surprise. You think it's not going to happen, and it does. The difficult part of receiving God's grace is maintaining a balance between thinking *I can do whatever I feel like doing because God's grace will cover it all*, and believing *Everything in my life—my success, my marriage, how my kids turn out, how whole I become—depends totally on what I do*. Neither extreme exemplifies grace and mercy, but people who have been emotionally damaged often fall into the latter category. They feel that if they don't achieve the perfection they think they should, they must beat themselves up for it. If we are merciless on ourselves, we have a harder time receiving mercy and showing mercy to someone else. And one of the stipulations for receiving emotional healing is showing mercy to others: "The merciful man does good for his own soul, but he who is cruel troubles his own flesh" (Proverbs 11:17). The Lord's mercies are "new every morning" (Lamentations 3:23), and so should ours be.

Pray the Scriptures

Jesus, I give You praise and thanksgiving for the grace that You have lavished on me. Father, I thank You because Your Word says that You will give more grace (James 4:6). I pray that I will give grace to others as freely as You have given it to me. Your Word says You give grace to the humble. I pray I will always humble myself before You so that I may continue to receive Your grace and mercy. I acknowledge it is not something that I can earn, but it is a gift from You.

Look over the scriptures you studied today and let them guide you as you write your own prayer below that addresses your specific needs.

A PRAYER TO
Receive and Embrace God's Love

Imagine someone giving you a present wrapped in shiny paper with an exquisite bow on top. You say, "Thank you so much for the gift. The paper is beautiful, the bow is breathtaking, and I will cherish it forever." Then you put the gift on the table and let it sit unopened. How sad it would be for both the giver and the recipient of the intended gift. And yet, how often does God bestow love on us and we refuse to receive and embrace it?

Key Scripture

"Behold what manner of love the Father has bestowed on us, that we should be called children of God!" (1 John 3:1).

Prepare to Pray

When Michael and I were married, I became financially secure for the first time. Even though my dad had worked hard all his life, he never made much money, and we always lived on the bare threads of existence. When he retired and moved to a farm in central California with my mother, his retirement didn't even cover the basic essentials. Michael and I tried to give them money periodically, but my mother wouldn't hear of it. One especially cold winter day I called them and found out they were both sick with serious chest colds. They had been freezing in their house for the past month because they didn't have enough money to buy fuel for the heater.

Here I was, with more than enough money to help, and they were suffering needlessly. I immediately made arrangements for a fuel delivery, and I realized how much our heavenly Father must be grieved at our needless suffering. I, too, forget that some things are my inheritance and my birthright because of Jesus. But I don't forget for very long anymore, because I know what God's gifts are and that they are there for me. I want you to know too.

Study the Scriptures

- Look up and read Romans 8:35–39. What does this passage reveal about God's love?

- Paul says that nothing can separate you from the love of Christ (verses 38–39). How does knowing God's love for you is unshakable impact your thoughts?

- In what ways do you struggle with grasping God's great love for you?

- Being convinced of God's love for you takes the pressure off you to find love and acceptance in other places. How might your life be different if you fully grasped the depth of God's love for you?

- Look up the following passages and consider how they relate to receiving God's love. How can you apply these truths to your own life?

Psalm 119:76–77	
Jeremiah 31:3–4	
John 14:23	
Romans 8:35	
Romans 8:38–39	

Respond to God's Word

Just as food helps us grow physically and education helps us grow mentally, it takes love for us to grow emotionally. If we aren't nurtured with love, our emotions stay immature, and we are always searching for the love we never had. But how do you ever get that love when the ones who are supposed to love you don't—or are not able to—communicate it to you?

In the flesh you'll try anything. At a certain level of need, any kind of attention—even negative—is better than no attention at all. We do and say things we shouldn't to gain attention, acceptance, and love from others. But in the Spirit, there is another way: receiving the love of God.

The Bible says, "The LORD's unfailing love surrounds the one who trusts in him" (Psalm 32:10 NIV). The more you say, "God, I trust Your love for me and all that You say in Your Word about me and my circumstances," the more you will experience God's love in your heart. Receiving the gift of God's love means that we don't have to do desperate things for approval. Nor do we have to be depressed when we don't receive love from other people exactly the way we feel we need it. When we sense God's love, it takes the pressure off relationships and frees us to be who we were made to be.

If you have doubts about God's love for you, ask Him to show it to you. Read what the Bible says about His love and choose to believe Him. The love of God is not just a feeling; it's God's Spirit. Because He is love, just spending time in His presence in prayer and praise causes His love to permeate your being. Opening up and receiving God's love makes you more able to love others, even people for whom you have no natural affinity. Radiating love toward others is part of perfecting God's love in you. It also causes people to love you more. This all brings emotional healing. God's love is always more than we expect. That's why we are brought to tears so often in His presence. They are tears of gratitude for love beyond our imagination!

Pray the Scriptures

Father, I know that You love me because You had Your Son die on the cross so I could be forgiven of my sins (John 3:16). You further showed Your love for me by making me a child of Yours (1 John 3:1). Lord, I pray that You will help me to get that information from my head down into my heart. I pray I would understand the depth of Your love for me so I won't look to other people and things to fill a void that only You can fill. Help me to understand that Your love for me isn't based on my performance, but on Your grace and goodness.

Look over the scriptures you studied today and let them guide you as you write your own prayer below that addresses your specific needs.

A PRAYER FOR
Overcoming Thoughts of Self-Harm or Suicide

When I was a teenager, I was so overcome with emotional torment that I could not envision a future. I felt ugly, worthless, stupid, unwanted, and unloved. I took an overdose of drugs, but it was not to attract attention or make people feel sorry for me. I didn't leave a note or phone for help. I simply did not want to wake up again.

The first lie we believe when we contemplate suicide is, *There is no other way out.* We believe that our situation is hopeless. Then we accept the lie that death is the only means of escape. In the Lord, these things are never true, no matter how painful and agonizing your circumstances. God in you is stronger than anything you are facing, and with Him comes freedom and deliverance.

Key Scripture

"I shall not die, but live,
And declare the works of the Lord" (Psalm 118:17).

Prepare to Pray

If you are suffering with thoughts of suicide, remember that those thoughts come from Satan. A desire to die is not from God and is not from you. You may want to be free of physical and emotional pain, and rightly so, but the thought of killing yourself to do it comes from a spirit of death sent from hell to destroy you. It is not you! The Spirit of God in you always has a solution that leads to life. If you are contemplating suicide, as I know some who read these pages may be, I want to tell you that I have been in the same bottomless pit you're in, and I've known the anguish, despair, and pain. And as someone who has come through that dark season, I plead with you to hold on because better days are coming.

Study the Scriptures

- Look up and read John 10:10. What did Jesus say are the three roles of the thief (Satan)?

- What did Jesus say His reason for coming is?

- What evidence does this passage reveal about where thoughts of suicide originate?

- Who is a trusted friend, neighbor, family member, or counselor you can talk to and ask to pray for you? If you don't know, ask God to show you someone.

- Look up the following passages and consider how they relate to thoughts of death and self-harm. How can you apply these truths to your prayers and self-talk?

Lamentations 3:22–23	
Proverbs 14:12	
Proverbs 14:26–27	
Psalm 116:1–7	

Respond to God's Word

Fortunately, I didn't take enough drugs to die, so I ended up sick instead of dead. When I did wake up, however, I felt different, even though nothing in my circumstances had changed. I wasn't sure why I had been spared from death, but somehow I didn't want to die anymore. Why my perception changed, I don't know. That's why it's important to remember, even in the midst of suicidal thoughts, that at any moment in our lives, things can change. In fact, change is inevitable. The only thing that doesn't change is God: "For I am the LORD, I do not change" (Malachi 3:6). God is always working on your behalf. You may feel at an all-time low right now, but tomorrow you could feel entirely different.

It's crucial that you resist thoughts of self-harm and don't entertain thoughts of death. If you allow yourself to think, *I don't want to live,* that type of thinking is dangerous. And don't think that because you have received Jesus you can get away with those thoughts either.

Never attempt to handle serious suicidal thoughts without help. In a crisis, seek out someone who can counsel you now—or call 9-1-1 or a suicide hotline. For long-term help, reach out to a Christian therapist or psychologist, a psychiatrist, a pastor, a counselor, a friend, or a strong believer in the Lord. Get together with other believers who can pray with you and for you, and make sure you go to church regularly for extensive times of worship and prayer. You must be built up from the inside and allow your circumstances to be transformed. If you kill yourself, you will never know the wonderful things that He has waiting for you. Why miss the greatest part of your life by ending it? Know that because Jesus lives, your life is worth living too. If you have to say the following prayer twenty times a day, do it.

Pray the Scriptures

God, I recognize my thoughts of suicide are not from You but they are from the Enemy. Satan comes to kill, steal, and destroy. Jesus, You came so that I can have abundant life (John 10:10). Father, I pray that You would deliver my feet from the snares of the Enemy (Psalm 91:3). Hide me in the shadow of Your wings (Psalm 17:8). Be my rock and refuge where I can always go (Psalm 71:3). Give me discernment and open my eyes to the truth. May I be quick to recognize the errors of my own thoughts. I submit my life to You. Lead me in the way You would have me to go. I want to live and glorify You, Father God. By the authority given to me in Jesus' name, I resist the spirit of suicide and refuse any voice that tells me I deserve to die. Thank You, Jesus, that You died to break every hold death wants to have on my life.

Look over the scriptures you studied today and let them guide you as you write your own prayer below that addresses your specific needs.

A PRAYER TO
Overcome Lust

Lust is an excessive desire to gratify any of the senses. The most common is sexual desire, but it is not the only one. Every lustful act begins as a simple thought. We are deceived if we think we are too strong or too good to ever be tempted by anything.

It's a mistake to believe that lustful sins are private and impact only you. Sins of lust often hurt other people, and destroy marriages, families, and reputations. Most of us don't think that our sins are against God. Yet God does suffer from our transgressions, and when we sin in any way we sin against God. Psalm 51:4 says, "Against You, You only, have I sinned, and done this evil in Your sight—that You may be found just when You speak, and blameless when You judge."

Key Scripture

"He who trusts in his own heart is a fool, but whoever walks wisely will be delivered" (Proverbs 28:26).

Prepare to Pray

People who believe they are immune to temptation are among those most at risk. You might be tempted to believe that you couldn't fall into the trap of lust. Maybe you've been happily married for years and it's never been a problem for you. Or perhaps you're a committed Christian and you can't imagine ever falling into sins of obsession. But history reveals all kinds of people have fallen into the trap of lust. The Bible tells us that King David was a man after God's own heart (1 Samuel 13:14). In other words, David loved God. David is a well-known personality in Scripture for good reason. He's known for killing the giant Goliath with a slingshot, and later becoming a dynamic king of Israel. Simply put, King David had everything in the world going for him. And yet he fell into the sin of lust.

Study the Scriptures

- Look up and read 2 Samuel 11–12. What stands out to you in this story?

- How did David's sin of lust negatively impact other people?

- **What consequences did David face?**

- **Is there a specific area where you are tempted by lust? What steps do you need to take to prevent yourself from falling into sin?**

- **Look up the following passages and consider how they relate to overcoming lust. How can you apply these truths to your own life?**

Proverbs 11:6	
Galatians 5:16–17	
Galatians 6:7–8	
1 Thessalonians 4:3–5	

Respond to God's Word

As you think about your own temptations, look at where David failed. First, King David was where he wasn't supposed to be; he should have been with his troops at Rabbah. Instead, he stayed home. Second, he probably imagined what it would be like to be with Bathsheba. He fell prey to the lie of lust: *It doesn't hurt to think about it if I'm not actually going to do anything.* This is why it's crucial to be intentional in what we allow ourselves to think about. Third, he may have thought, *This won't really hurt anyone else, and I will be truly happy,* but the future proved him wrong. Pitfall of lust. Scripture says, "Do not be deceived, God is not mocked; for whatever a man sows, that he will also reap" (Galatians 6:7). God punished David severely and several others suffered from David's sin, one that began with a wrong thought.

Thankfully, David finally came to his senses and confessed and repented of his sin (Psalm 51). If you find yourself in a pit of sin you can do the same. It's never too late to confess your sin to God and turn away from it. The sooner the better. And the Lord will also forgive our sin, just as He forgave David's. God does not, however, take away the consequences of our actions. Someone who is truly repentant can help others who seem to be straying toward the same pitfall. And you can too. Ask God to show you how you can serve Him in this way.

And if you have acted on a spirit of lust, you need to receive deliverance. Get help. Go to a counselor, a Christian therapist, a pastor, or a strong believer who will keep your confidence. Confess your sin. Then experience the joy of being forgiven. David wrote Psalm 32 to express his renewed relationship with God: "Blessed is he whose transgression is forgiven, whose sin is covered. Blessed is the man to whom the Lord does not impute iniquity, and in whose spirit there is no deceit" (verses 1–2).

Pray the Scriptures

Almighty Father, help me not sin against you even in thought. Create in me a clean heart, O God, and renew a steadfast spirit within me (Psalm 51:10). Help me to walk wisely so I will always be delivered from every thought that is not of You (Proverbs 28:26). Your Word says that the temptations I deal with are common to mankind. Your Word says You are faithful and will not allow me to be tempted without providing a way of escape (1 Corinthians 10:13). Cause my thoughts to be glorifying to You, and help me always to accept Your way of escape. Keep me far away from lustful thoughts of any kind.

Look over the scriptures you studied today and let them guide you as you write your own prayer below that addresses your specific needs.

A PRAYER FOR
Overcoming Perfectionism

Chasing perfection is like living your life like a hamster on a wheel. You'll exhaust yourself and never arrive at your destination. The pursuit of perfection can creep into any part of life. People who are part of the entertainment industry in Hollywood, as I was, try to look perfect every time they walk out of the house. I certainly tried to do that, and I fell into the pit of perfectionism. But perfectionism might show up in your workplace, how you keep your house, raise your kids, or how you present yourself in public settings or on social media. Chasing perfection increased my fearfulness. I was afraid of marriage because I thought I wouldn't be a perfect wife. I was afraid to have children because I thought I wouldn't be a perfect mom. For years I wouldn't write anything for people to see because I feared what I wrote would not be perfect. I was trying to be perfect in order to be acceptable to myself and to others; but in reality, the more perfect we try to make ourselves, the more uncomfortable we make the people around us. The deception of perfectionism is in thinking that anyone other than God can ever be perfect. God knows our actions can never be perfect. That's why He sent Jesus. He is perfect.

Key Scripture

"Not that I have already attained, or am already perfected; but I press on, that I may lay hold of that for which Christ Jesus has also laid hold of me" (Philippians 3:12).

Prepare to Pray

The apostle Paul, the greatest evangelist of all time, did not think he was perfect. He said, "Not that I have already attained, or am already perfected; but I press on, that I may lay hold of that for which Christ Jesus has also laid hold of me" (Philippians 3:12). He also acknowledged his struggle to do what was right: "For what I am doing, I do not understand. For what I will to do, that I do not practice; but what I hate, that I do . . . For I know that in me (that is, in my flesh) nothing good dwells" (Romans 7:15, 18). If the apostle Paul, who gave his life for Christ, knew he was not perfect, why do we think we can be—or should be?

Study the Scriptures

- Look up and read Romans 3:10–12. According to Paul, why is the pursuit of excellence unattainable?

- God knows that all people sin and fall short of His glory (Romans 3:23) and yet He sent His Son to die on the cross, so we'd have a Savior for our sins. How does this reality speak to your attitude about perfection?

- In what areas are you drawn toward perfectionism?

- In light of the passages you've read today, what steps do you need to take to let go of any pursuit of perfectionism? Ask God to show you if you are not sure.

- Look up the following passages and consider how they relate to perfection. How can you apply these truths to your own life?

Isaiah 64:6	
2 Corinthians 12:9	
Galatians 3:3	
1 John 1:8	

Do you struggle with perfectionism? Check the statements below to see if this is a pitfall for you:

- ☐ "I find it very hard to take criticism of my work."
- ☐ "If I can't do something well, I don't do it at all."
- ☐ "I feel ashamed if I show weakness or foolish behavior."
- ☐ "In my experience, if you want something done right, you have to do it yourself."
- ☐ "I get upset when things don't go as planned."
- ☐ "I think about my failures much more than my successes."
- ☐ "I sometimes think other people dwell on my faults, rather than my strengths."

Respond to God's Word

God says He wants to make you something more than your human excellence can ever be. He wants to love you into wholeness. You will rise to the level and degree that you sense His love in your life. That's why I no longer worry about being perfect, because the perfection of Christ is manifested by His love flowing through me. When you look in the mirror and see the excellence of Jesus reflected back, that's when you will have a sense of your true worth. The actual transformation takes place every time you worship the Lord for His perfection. Never forget Paul's admonition to the Hebrew Christians: "For the law made nothing perfect" (Hebrews 7:19 NIV); so realize that your striving will make nothing perfect. Only the perfection of Jesus in you will perfect you.

Pray the Scriptures

Lord, I do not want to struggle with perfection, so if there is any in me, show me and I will confess it as sin (1 John 1:9). God, I know that only You are perfect. Help me to remember that because You are perfect, I don't have to be. Help me to overcome any need I have to be approved of by others. I pray that I will not get caught up in seeking others' approval so that I can focus solely on living my life in a way that is pleasing to You. Thank you for your mercy and grace that enables me to do so much more than I could ever do without You. Help me to be more like You every day. I pray that You, Jesus, who has begun a good work in me, will continue to complete it until I see you in heaven (Philippians 1:6).

Look over the scriptures you studied today and let them guide you as you write your own prayer below that addresses your specific needs.